Read Me First!

A Style Guide for the Computer Industry

Sun Technical Publications

Printed in the United States of America

10 9 8 7 6 5 4 3 2 1

ISBN 0-13-455347-0

SunSoft Press
A Prentice Hall Title

Connie Skoog

Contents

≡

6. Mechanics of Writing   67

7. Technical Abbreviations, Acronyms, and Units of Measurement   97

B. Developing a Publications Department   189

C. Checklists and Forms 221

Read Me First!

Acknowledgments ≡

Read Me First! A Style Guide for the Computer Industry is a documentation style guide based substantially on *Sun Microsystems Editorial Style Guide*.

Those who worked on *Read Me First! A Style Guide for the Computer Industry* are Project Lead: Janice Gelb; Project Editor: Mary Martyak; Authors: James Brook, Jeffrey Gardiner, Janice Gelb, Cindy Hall, John Hevelin, Charles Jackson, Billie Markim, Mary Martyak, Jean McVey, Diane Plampin, PJ Schemenaur, and Linnea Wickstrom.

Those who worked on the second edition of *Sun Microsystems Editorial Style Guide* are Anne Alexander, Bruce Bartlett, Michael Bierman, James Brook, Stephanie Brucker, Janice Gelb, Cindy Hall, Charles Jackson, James Langdell, Billie Markim, Mary McInnis, and Linda Wiesner.

Those who developed the original *Sun Microsystems Editorial Style Guide* are Niklass Andersson, Bruce Bartlett, Michael Bierman, Stephanie Brucker, David Damkoehler, Will Doherty, Eduardo Gutentag, James Langdell, Andrea Marra, Susan Najour, Joyce Uggla, Linda Wiesner, and Janice Winsor.

Special thanks go to the members of the Sun Microsystems Editorial Forum, who served as primary reviewers and architects of all versions of *Sun Microsystems Editorial Style Guide*, and to Andrea Marra, who had the original concept and was the driving force behind the original book.

We'd also like to thank our publishers: Karin Ellison and Rachel Borden of SunSoft Press and Greg Doench of Prentice Hall PTR.

Note – An earlier version of Chapter 4, "Writing for an International Audience," originally appeared in *Sun Microsystems Editorial Style Guide*, and subsequently in *Solaris International Developer's Guide* by Bill Tuthill (New Jersey: SunSoft Press/ Prentice Hall, 1993).

Preface

≡

i stands for information, and *Read Me First! A Style Guide for the Computer Industry* provides everything you always wanted to know about documenting computer products—from style pointers to legal guidelines, from writing for an international audience to developing a documentation department.

Accompanying *Read Me First!* is a CD-ROM disc containing a version of the book viewable on line with FrameViewer® and HTML files that enable you to view the book through a Web browser, as well as FrameMaker® templates for book creation complete with paragraph and character tags. See "Starting the CD-ROM" at the back of this book for details on how to start the CD-ROM disc.

How This Book Is Organized

Read Me First! contains the following:

Chapter 1, "Understanding Style," examines the "personality" of effective writing style that publications professionals have acquired in the computer industry.

Chapter 2, "Working With an Editor," explains how writers and editors can work together to produce high-quality documentation.

Chapter 3, "Working With Illustrations," provides information about incorporating illustrations, proper use of callouts and leader lines, and working with an illustrator.

Chapter 4, "Writing for an International Audience," provides guidelines for writing material that can be translated easily into other languages.

Chapter 5, "Legal Guidelines," contains information about copyrights and trademarks.

Chapter 6, "Mechanics of Writing," reviews basic punctuation rules and guidelines, capitalization, contractions, and use of numbers and numerals.

Chapter 7, "Technical Abbreviations, Acronyms, and Units of Measurement," gives rules for using abbreviations and acronyms, and contains a table of some common terms used in the computer industry.

Chapter 8, "Constructing Text," offers guidelines for setting up elements in documents, such as section heads; tables; lists; cross-references; Notes, Cautions, and Warnings; graphical user interfaces; and typographic conventions.

Chapter 9, "Indexing," covers issues such as selecting topics to index, style rules for creating an index, and editing an index.

Appendix A, "Recommended Reading," presents a list of books, divided by subject headings, that you may want to refer to for additional information.

Appendix B, "Developing a Publications Department," provides information about issues related to a documentation department, including topics such as scheduling, roles and responsibilities, technical review, and printing and production.

Appendix C, "Checklists and Forms," contains sample checklists that you can use at various stages of documentation development, including editing coverage, art tracking, and a technical review cover letter.

Understanding Style   1 ≡

If *content* is *what* we communicate, then *style* is *how* we communicate that content. Writing style is determined by all the decisions you make while creating a document, such as the type and tone of information you present, choice of words, language and format consistency, use of technical terms, and so forth. Your style is part of the unique value that writers add to the product. In the literary world, style is judged in part on artistic grounds, which may be highly subjective. In the field of technical documentation, however, experience and practice have provided objective criteria for evaluating style.

This chapter presents some guidelines for writing effectively and refers you to additional sources of information. It discusses:

- The importance of an effective writing style
- Stylistic principles
- How to improve your style

Why Is Style Important?

Good style is synonymous with effective communication. Effective communication is not some abstract academic goal to be achieved for its own sake. Documents that communicate effectively reduce your company's costs and increase customer satisfaction, both effects resulting in increased profits. Customer satisfaction increases when accurate and functional documentation enables your customer to use your product quickly and efficiently. A document written in a style that responds to the requirements of its readers also results in fewer revisions, fewer calls to customer support, reduced training needs, and easier translation.

1

Some Stylistic Principles

There is extensive literature on good writing style, and this chapter is not intended to duplicate that literature. However, there are a few stylistic issues to discuss that relate directly to computer documentation.

In general, two principles underly these stylistic considerations:

- *Time is a valuable commodity* – Readers of computer documentation are generally in a hurry. They have turned to the documentation to find answers to problems and are justifiably impatient to get on with the task at hand. Anything that impedes the customers' speedy understanding is bad style.

- *Readers are worldwide* – Foreign markets are a significant source of revenue for manufacturers of computer products, and more frequently than ever before, documentation is being translated into languages other than English.

Write Simply, Directly, and Accurately

Straightforward, uncluttered writing is easier to understand and translate than more convoluted text. Keep sentences and syntax simple. Use short, familiar words. Respect a reader's level of technical knowledge and competency and make sure that your writing does not convey an arrogant or patronizing tone.

A reader expects you to be an expert on the subject or product discussed in your document. Write in a style that affirms your expertise. For example, too many sentences that include "you can" or "it is recommended" may confuse a reader who asks "but *should* I do this?" Instead, use imperative verbs that tell a reader accurately and concisely what to do. If you explain that a choice exists, describe for a reader the advantages and disadvantages of the alternatives, and make recommendations depending upon different scenarios.

Avoid Humor

One of the great temptations for writers of computer documentation is the urge to inject a note of levity into the text to relieve a reader's (or author's) uneasiness with the material. This temptation should be resisted—even genuinely humorous commentary is a distraction and will become annoying on subsequent readings. Many attempts at humor are likely to fail outright. Likewise, humor that descends into "user-friendly chumminess" never works. A sympathetic reader may forgive you for trying to "lighten up" the text, while another reader may resent a cloying tone.

For example, you might think that all readers will enjoy this humor injected into a tutorial:

> You can use a mouse (one without fur) with the window environment on your computer.

However, "one without fur" detracts from the content of the sentence and distracts a reader.

Most importantly, humor is difficult (if not impossible) to translate successfully. Humor is strictly cultural; what may be funny to Americans could be obscene to readers in another country.

Avoid Jargon

Writers frequently incorporate jargon associated with the subject matter into their documentation, in part to demonstrate their mastery of the subject, and in part because jargon adds "color" to documentation. This is another temptation that you should resist.

Jargon can be difficult for "non-initiates" to understand and will impede comprehension. Jargon also can be ambiguous; different fields of expertise can interpret the same jargon in different ways. Finally, jargon can be very difficult to translate.

For examples, the words listed below can be interpreted as valid computer terms or jargon used in the industry. If you use them, make sure that you, and the reader, understand their context and meaning in your document.

- argument
- boot
- bring up
- bundle
- client
- command
- comment out
- dataless
- default
- diskfull
- diskless
- end user
- enter
- execute
- floppy
- getting help
- help facility
- interoperability
- make up
- mount
- option
- power up/down
- server
- string

1

Be Consistent

Consistency is not just some abstract goal to be achieved for its own sake; rather, the intention is to reduce the impact of the mechanics of communication on readers. Readers project some significance onto every change in tone, language, or typographic convention you use. A consistent style enables readers to internalize the language and text conventions of a document so that understanding occurs on an almost subliminal basis, and so that truly significant points stand out more clearly. This is one of the most valuable aspects of good style. Refer to Chapter 8, "Constructing Text," for consistency guidelines.

Anticipate a Reader's Questions

One of the most important contributions a writer makes is to anticipate a reader's questions and provide appropriate answers. As the subject expert, a writer can create a climate of understanding that is far more significant than merely recounting facts about the product.

For example, when you review a procedure in your document with a reader's perspective in mind, ask these questions:

- What assumptions have I made about what the reader knows?
- Do steps follow in a logical sequence? Are there any gaps in the instructions?
- Are even the simplest words used precisely? For example, did I write "any" when I meant "all"?
- Did I define all technical terms?
- Have I incorrectly put conceptual and explanatory material within steps, rather than in paragraph text?

Avoid Sexist Language

Regarding the issue of sexism in language—appearances count.

Writers who could never be described as sexist must be careful that their writing does not convey sexism. Equal opportunity in the workplace means that not all roles are filled by men. However, language has developed so that "men" often refers to "men and women," and that "he," "him," and "his" are regarded by some people as gender-neutral words. In decades past, this sentence would have been perfectly acceptable:

Ask your system administrator for his advice.

Today, the consistent usage of "he" and "his" is far less acceptable. These pronouns carry too much assumption about the sex of an individual. Writers who defend using such pronouns must contemplate this: Many readers will interpret a writer's intentions negatively, and consciously or subconsciously reject the work.

Your creative challenge is to eliminate not only the real sexism, but also the perceived sexism, from your writing. Stylistically, there are some boundaries.

Acceptable Methods of Achieving Common Gender

Consider the following suggestions as ways to achieve common gender:

- Write plural antecedents and pronouns as often as possible.

  Awkward: Tell each user to shut down his machine.

  Better: Tell the users to shut down their machines.

- Eliminate the possessive as much as possible when you're writing in the third person.

  Awkward: Ask your system administrator for his advice.

  Better: Ask your system administrator for advice.

- Use the word "you."

  Awkward: If the user decides he wants to change the settings . . . .

  Better: If you want to change the settings . . . .

- Instead of using a personal pronoun, repeat its antecedent—when doing so doesn't sound unpleasant or unnatural (distance between occurrences of the noun usually helps).

  Awkward: If a system administrator installed the software, wait until he can help you.

  Better: If a system administrator installed the software that you're having trouble with, wait until the administrator can help you.

Consider the following suggestions as somewhat daring:

- Give names to "third persons."

  This technique won't work for all types of documentation, but it can be effective in a tutorial or other type of user's guide. Consider naming names—obviously male or female—to humanize your writing and eliminate the "he or she" clumsiness.

For example, if you want to tell a user how to copy a file from someone else's directory, try this:

> Before you can copy a file from someone else's directory—Sally Smith's, for example—you need permission. Ask Smith to set her file permissions to grant you access. After she has changed permissions, you are free to copy the file.

- Create your own techniques, keeping in mind that writing has to sound natural, has to be taken literally, and has to inform. Don't settle for inoffensiveness if you can also be enlightening.

Unacceptable Methods of Achieving Common Gender

Eliminating the appearance of sexism by writing poorly, ungrammatically, or self-consciously is not a good tradeoff. Keep the following in mind:

- There is no such being as a "s/he." Never write it.
- "Their" relates only to a plural antecedent. "Ask your system administrator for their advice" is just plain wrong.
- The "his or her" gambit is grammatically correct, but unnatural.
- Even in pursuit of the fine goal of eliminating perceived sexism, never dehumanize people with the pronoun "it."

How to Improve Your Style

An effective writing style is not acquired magically—you can improve your style through study, practice, and constructive criticism. The elements of good technical writing are not mysterious unknowns; good style can be learned.

Study Good Writing

An excellent way to improve your style is to read and study good writing. Appendix A, "Recommended Reading," lists several dozen books worthy of your professional attention. Study the literature in your area of specialization—what works? what doesn't? why?

As you analyze examples of effective technical writing, you'll find that the writers delivered appropriate information by presenting the material:

- When the reader needed it and in a logical progression
- Where the reader expected to find it
- In a tone and with language that the reader could immediately understand
- In a consistent form that the reader could easily interpret

Work With an Editor

If you are fortunate enough to work at a site with an editorial staff, take every opportunity to have your work edited. A good editor is an invaluable partner in producing effective documentation. Your editor is the expert in your company's style and can often assist you in determining the best way to present your information to the customer.

A good editor will be familiar not only with other documentation produced at your company, but also with other documentation in your field, including that of your competitors. An editor relates to a document as an advocate for a reader, as a professional who can critique your work, and often is the "first customer" to read your document. Refer to Chapter 2, "Working With an Editor," for further discussion of the writer-editor partnership.

Attend Classes and Training

Technical writing is a recognized profession. An excellent way to improve your style is to attend classes offered by other professionals in the field. Classes are made available by:

- Colleges and university extension programs
- In-house training services
- Commercial seminars and tutorials

1

Read Me First!

Working With an Editor 2

Writing computer documentation involves converting a hodgepodge of information supplied by engineers and marketing professionals into a useful, well-written document. The final document often is a result of efforts from the entire publications team, including writer, editor, designer, illustrator, and production coordinator. However, the content of the document is most closely developed through the work of writer and editor.

This chapter discusses:

- The role of an editor
- Types of editorial review
- Planning ahead for editing
- Submitting a document for editing
- Creating a style sheet
- Editing marks

Role of an Editor

An editor helps a writer to focus on content and effective presentation and provides another set of eyes to check all details. An editor's primary goal, as stated by Robert Bly and Gary Blake in *Technical Writing Structure, Standards and Style* (McGraw-Hill, 1982), is "to help the reader by making publications easier, less time-consuming, and more enjoyable to read."

The partnership of writer and editor produces easy-to-use, high-quality, effective documents. One writer explains:

> A savvy writer knows that a good editor is an indispensable ally. By approaching your work as a customer would, the editor is able to provide you with insight on how your work is likely to be received and interpreted. At the same time, the editor is able to restore the freshness of perspective that the writer necessarily loses while working on the same manual day in and day out.

2

Any editor is concerned with use of language, flow, tone, grammar, punctuation, capitalization, spelling, sentence structure, consistency, and so forth. However, a *technical editor* also is concerned with technical content, compatibility of the technical depth with the reader's background, effective communication of technical information, consistent use of technical terms and symbols, and competent coordination of text and artwork.

By marking something and suggesting an alternative, an editor indicates to a writer that the original may be, for example, misleading, awkward, imprecise, confusing, or incomplete.

One staff technical writer, who also writes books for trade publishers, described an editing experience:

> My most recent "noncompany" editor edited a book I wrote. He didn't cross out one word. He didn't change anything stylistically. Instead, he made suggestions about what should be added, what could be made more clear, what the reader would want to know—hundreds of suggestions that greatly improved the quality of the book.
>
> The editor and I were both professionals, each with our own set of skills. We worked together to create a product that received extremely favorable reviews in the popular press.
>
> Too often it is impossible for writers to be objective about their own writing. As the first reader of a writer's work, the editor is in an important position to elevate the quality of that work. Writer and editor, together, should come to an understanding of what relationship will produce the best possible quality of writing.

Types of Editing

A document may undergo more than one editorial review, each for a different purpose. The type of edit the manual gets usually depends upon where it is in the product cycle. For example, a *developmental edit* of the manual would occur early in the cycle, around the pre-alpha test or alpha time frame when there may be more time to address issues such as organization and structure. A *copy edit* is best during the beta review, when the manual is more complete and stable. Before it goes to press, the book should receive a *proofreading*.

Developmental Editing

Developmental editing is hard to define because its functions depend upon the documentation set or book under consideration. You can think of developmental editing as a phase in the production of a document rather than a series of discrete tasks. It is the phase when restructuring of a set or a book, reorganization of chapters or sections, and major rewriting (or suggestions for rewriting) should be done. The issues the editor raises during a developmental edit can affect the character of subsequent sections or chapters of a document, especially if the edit is done on a sample chapter or an early draft of a manual. A developmental editor assesses the overall focus and direction of the manual. Some global copy editing issues may be raised at this time, especially when they provide the writer with examples of style or word usage. See "Developmental Editing Checklist" in Appendix C, "Checklists and Forms," for the items reviewed during a developmental edit.

Copy Editing

The editor does minimal rewriting, if any, during a copy edit because issues regarding structure and organization have been addressed throughout the developmental edit. At the copy editing stage the editor performs two kinds of review: *mechanical editing* and *editing for house style*. Mechanical editing addresses such issues as punctuation, capitalization, subject-verb agreement, and so forth. Editing for house style involves interpreting and applying the strictures of house style. The editor also reads for correct usage of fonts, word processor tags, or other markup; structural elements (for example, tables, illustrations, lists); and the like. The best time for a copy edit, also called a *line edit*, is before or during the beta review. See "Copy Editing Checklist" in Appendix C, "Checklists and Forms," for the items reviewed during a copy edit.

Proofreading

Proofreading is the last step that writers and editors can take to ensure further quality. It involves one final scan of the document for errors that may have been overlooked in previous reviews. The writer also may have introduced new mistakes when incorporating new technical material or editorial comments. The proofreader's primary responsibility is to make sure that typographical errors, incorrect font usage, and formatting mistakes have not crept into the document. See "Proofreading Checklist" in Appendix C, "Checklists and Forms," for the items reviewed during a proofreading pass.

Planning Ahead for Editing

Writers should allocate time for editing when creating the documentation plan. The nature of the document and the schedule will determine how much editing is possible. See "Scheduling" in Appendix B, "Developing a Publications Department," for more details.

Consider these points:

- You can involve the editor as early as the research stage. The editor can help you with research on how similar products are handled and who the audience is.

- The editor can help you prepare your documentation plan. Consult the editor if you want advice on overall organization. Go over your editing needs with the editor and include editing cycles in the schedule.

- The alpha review is a good time for a full developmental edit. Beta review is usually too late to make the kinds of changes that may come out of a developmental edit.

- A copy edit at the beta review can clean up grammar, spelling, and conformance to your company's style standards.

- Proofreading at first customer ship (FCS) provides one last check for formatting issues and typos.

Your manager should maintain an editing schedule for your writing group, which is submitted regularly to the editor assigned to your group. As your submission date or other information (such as page count) changes from the information in the documentation plan, you should let your manager know so that the updated information can be included in the group editing schedule.

Submitting a Document for Editing

Before submitting a document for editing:

- Run your word processor's spelling checker.
- Check cross-references.
- Include or indicate placement of graphics.

The document you submit should be accompanied by a Request for Editing form (see "Request for Editing" in Appendix C, "Checklists and Forms"). This form supplies information such as your name and phone number, the stage of the document (alpha, beta, FCS), the name of the set to which the document belongs, and other information relevant to the editor.

Creating a Style Sheet

Maintaining a *style sheet* can help you keep track of special spelling, terminology, punctuation, capitalization, and other word or formatting usage.

A style sheet is the place where you and the editor can log the decisions made about product names, numbers, abbreviations and acronyms, hyphenation, and capitalization. If the document you are writing or editing is part of a set, using a style sheet helps maintain consistency among the various books.

When you create a style sheet, remember to pass it on to others who may benefit from it—writers of related documents, editors, illustrators, and production specialists. For a sample style sheet form, see "Editorial Style Sheet" in Appendix C, "Checklists and Forms."

Editing Marks

Table 2-1 shows standard editing and proofreading marks.

Table 2-1   Editing and Proofreading Marks

Mark	Explanation	Example
	Delete a letter	rabbitt
	Close up	upper case
	Delete a letter and close up	balloon
	Delete a word and close up	over the the river
	Insert a character	into te woods
	Insert an apostrophe	the cats meow
	Insert brackets	date ddmmyy
	Insert a colon	at 10 35
	Insert a comma	red yellow, and blue
	Insert an ellipsis mark	And so it goes
	Insert an em dash	We are all alike on the inside
	Insert an en dash	pages 4 10
	Insert a hyphen	reelect
	Insert parentheses	see page 97
	Insert a period	all done
	Insert quotation marks	Eureka!
	Insert a semicolon	...agree however, I object.

Table 2-1   Editing and Proofreading Marks (Continued)

Mark	Explanation	Example
≡	Capitalize a letter	<u>sun</u>
≡	Capitalize a word	<u>unix</u>
/	Lowercase a letter	S/un
/	Lowercase a word	/WORKSTATION
◯	Spell out a number (or use numerals)	④ (forty)
⊐	Move to the right	move over some!
⊏	Move to the left	now you are too far over
⊐ ⊏	Center	⊐smack in the middle⊏
(bf)	Use boldface type	make me bold(bf)
(ital)	Use italics	make me italic(ital)
(tr)	Transpose letters or words	word proecssor
⌐	Break line here	end of line start new line here
⌣	Join two lines	join these two lines together
¶	Begin a new paragraph	¶ One thought. Starting another.
stet	Leave as originally written	never editors ~~make~~ mistakes
(wf)	Wrong font	worksta(tion)

Working With Illustrations 3≡

A good illustration not only transmits dense and complex information at a glance, but it also helps a reader to retain more information. Combining text and images focuses attention and helps a reader filter data quickly for specific information. As documentation moves on line, you may find yourself in the role of a screenwriter or director as you blend text, still images, video, audio, and animation in on-line multimedia documents.

This chapter discusses:

- Working with an illustrator
- Illustration formats, styles, and types
- Writing and arranging callouts
- Using leader lines

Working With an Illustrator

Even if you're a writer who can double as an illustrator, there are good reasons why you shouldn't do your own illustrations:

- Drawing is not an economical use of your time—time spent drawing is time not spent writing.

- A drawing created by an illustrator can be archived for use by all writers.

- Documentation benefits from enhanced visual coherency and consistency across the entire library if all the artwork is done by the department illustrators.

- An illustrator provides more resources than just drawings. An illustrator can help you hone your ideas, pinpoint where drawings would be most effective in your document, and review the finished graphics for accuracy.

Writers and illustrators are part of a team, collaborating to produce a manual with seamlessly integrated text and graphics. This teamwork is enhanced by involving an illustrator as early as possible in the development cycle of your document.

Schedule a meeting with an illustrator as soon as you have an idea of the number and types of illustrations you need. Try to provide the illustrator with reference materials to use when creating the drawings: hard-copy printouts of existing drawings, a hand-drawn sketch, a piece of hardware, a photograph, and so on. (See "Illustration and Graphics Design" in Appendix B, "Developing a Publications Department," for a suggested graphics design process.)

Illustration as Design

Illustration serves two functions in technical documentation: It clarifies the text and it imparts visual coherency and consistency.

Illustrations (sometimes called *figures* in technical documentation) improve the readability of a document. When confronted by many pages, a reader will find the manual less intimidating if the pages are broken up with illustrations. Figure 3-1 shows an example of how an illustration can make a page look less dense, without necessarily reducing the information available to a reader.

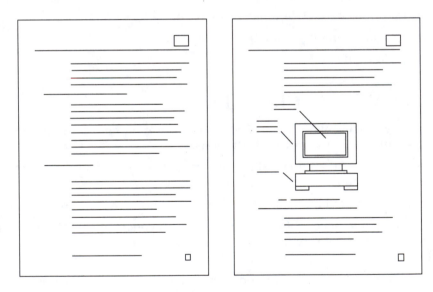

Figure 3-1   Page Layouts, With and Without an Illustration

An effective illustration can help guide a reader through a complex maze of concepts, descriptions, and instructions. No one wants to spend more time reading a manual than necessary, and an illustration can soften and simplify the technology for a reader, regardless of level of expertise.

Finally, a carefully crafted illustration should not be constrained by language or culture when your document is translated for international use.

Using Illustrations

Figures can be any type of useful illustration, such as conceptual diagrams of remote procedure calls, detailed line drawings, terminal screen captures, flowcharts, clip art, cartoons, icons, or photographs of hardware.

Illustrations are most effective when describing:

- *Objects* – Hardware, icons, and screen captures
- *Actions* – Adding or removing parts, or interactions between moving parts
- *Processes* – Flowcharts, schematics, graphs, and numbers
- *Concepts* – Blueprints, maps, and hypertext structures

You can use illustrations not only to describe objects, processes, actions, and concepts, but also to set a tone for the entire book. By careful selection of nontechnical drawings for part divider pages, for example, you can help guide a reader through the book, emphasize a teamwork process, or make a potentially dull subject more inviting and accessible. Stylistically, this can lighten your document or give it a visual grace it might otherwise lack.

Planning Placement of Illustrations

Where you place illustrations on the page can cue a reader where to look next or visually link different ideas through the use of different line weights, different styles, subject matter, glyphs, and colors. For ideas on ways to place illustrations with a smooth visual flow in mind, look through comic books or illustrated children's stories and see how the writers and artists worked together to lead you around the pages. While comic books and children's stories may seem unlikely resources for technical documentation, they are excellent examples of effective collaboration between writers and illustrators, and demonstrate how different skills combine to present the flow of information.

Writing Captions for Illustrations

When writing *figure captions*, some writers choose to number and caption all figures in a document, while others use only a caption. Some writers elect not to caption figures when their context is so clear that captions would be redundant. Often screen captures that are discussed in the nearby paragraph text fit into the last category.

Use a figure caption, or number and caption, whenever you cross-reference figures in your document and when you want to compile a list of figures in the contents. Style consistency is important.

When you write a figure number and caption:

- Refer to the figure in the preceding text, and avoid introducing the figure with a phrase ending with a colon.

  Make sure that you introduce the context of the figure to the reader. Use the figure number when referring to the figure in text ("Figure 1-1 shows . . . .") rather than its position ("The figure below shows . . . ."). This will eliminate awkward text if your page break forces the figure onto the next page.

- Number the figure sequentially.

  You can use a single-digit numbering system (Figure 1, Figure 2, and so forth) that continues throughout the document; don't restart at Figure 1 at the beginning of a new chapter. Or, you can use a double-digit numbering system (Figure 1-1, Figure 2-1, and so forth) that uses the chapter number as the first digit and restarts at -1 for the first figure at the beginning of each chapter.

- Use the same capitalization style for figure captions as you use for section heads.

- Don't start a figure caption with an article (say "File Menu" rather than "The File Menu").

Adding Illustrations to a Document

How you add illustrations to your document depends upon the type of desktop publishing software you are using. Usually, you will either import existing illustrations into your document file or supply a new illustration. Either way, it is often very efficient to use separate text files and graphics files. In this way, you can continue to work on your text if you don't have the illustration ready, or if someone else is preparing the illustrations.

In general:

- Set up a separate file or directory for illustrations.

  Work in the illustration file while you prepare the illustration; for example, you may want to add callouts, or scale, resize, or crop the figure.

- Insert space in your document for the illustration, and its number and caption, to mark where the illustration will be displayed.

- Limit the number of figure sizes you use, and specify the alignment of figures in your document.

  Develop an art grid, which will help ensure consistent sizing and placement of figures. Often three figure size options and three alignment options are sufficient.

- Add callouts and leader lines to the figure.

  Callouts are text elements that clarify the illustration or provide readers with additional information or instructions. Callouts help connect the figure to the text. Keep the terms and descriptions in the callouts simple and concise. Use a consistent font for callouts, consistent alignment, and consistent capitalization and punctuation.

  Leader lines point from the callouts to specific parts of the illustration. Use a consistent point size for the leader line, and limit the alignment, length, and angle options for the lines.

- Merge the text and graphics files.

- Check that each figure is in the correct space.

Illustration Formats, Styles, and Types

This section describes the basics of the formats, styles, and types of illustration.

- *Formats* establish how files are recognized and handled by the computer and the printer—file types such as `.epsi` and TIFF.

- *Styles* are broad categories of illustration, such as 2-D, 3-D, and photographic.

- *Types* include data processes, line drawings, concept drawings, screen captures, cartoons, icons, and glyphs.

Illustration Formats

Most of the images displayed on computer monitors fall into two categories:

- *Object-oriented images* are based on mathematical formulas that enable you to resize the images easily and with no distortion. Objects include different elements, such as straight lines, curved shapes, and Bezier curves. PostScript™ format is the industry standard for handling type and line art images.

- *Bitmapped images* are formed of a rectangular arrangement of pixels. A value is assigned each pixel, ranging from 1 bit per pixel for black-and-white to 24 bits per pixel for full-color display. Often, images intended solely for on-line use, such as icons, are bitmapped images. All images are converted into bitmaps when sent from a computer to a printer. Bitmapped graphics are also called *raster graphics*.

Common formats for illustrations for technical documentation are:

- *Encapsulated PostScript (EPS)*, which is a common file format that enables a PostScript image to be placed in most desktop publishing files and rotated, resized, or otherwise manipulated.

- *Tag Image File Format (TIFF)*, which is a set of standards describing raster files that enables easy exchange of black-and-white, grayscale, and color images produced by different graphics programs on different platforms. For example, an image created in a paint program on a Macintosh® computer can be read by a paint program on a Sun™ workstation.

Illustration Styles

There are four common styles of illustration used in computer documents:

- *Isometric drawings* are a type of perspective drawing often used in engineering manuals. The mathematical structure puts all lines at angles of 30, 60, or 90 degrees.

- *3-D drawings* are on-line images designed to be viewed from all angles. Typically, you can rotate, bisect, and scale these images.

- *2-D drawings* are the most common style of illustration. They may be drawn in perspective, depending upon the subject matter.

- *Photographic, video stills,* and *animation* are styles that are appropriate for on-line use.

However, you do not have to reserve animation for films or on-line documents; you can use animation effectively in any printed form. Figure 3-2 is an example of animation showing how to unpack a shipping carton.

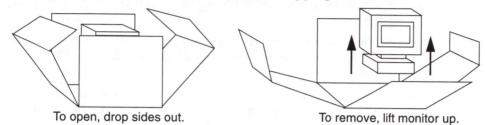

To open, drop sides out.   To remove, lift monitor up.

Figure 3-2   Illustrating an Animated Procedure

Illustration Types

Illustrations can be broken down into these main types:

- *Hardware line drawings* are common in technical manuals. Examples include black-and-white line drawings of disk drives, drawings of "exploded" SCSI ports, and drawings of people installing SIMMs. Line drawings can be shown in 3-D, 2-D, isometric, and other styles.

- *Clip art* is "generic" art that you can use as-is or in combination with other graphics. The subject matter is fairly nonspecific; for example, a picture of a monitor rather than an illustration of a specific, identifiable monitor.

- *Icons* and *glyphs* are visual cues that represent an object (such as hardware or an application's window), a process (such as an application), or a structure (such as a network).

  Icons are interactive and are used on line. They are small, mnemonic graphic images that serve as visual placeholders for a larger object or process.

/bin/csh

Figure 3-3   Icon

  Glyphs are noninteractive symbols that convey easily recognized information, often without using text. Examples of glyphs include the lightning bolt set inside a triangle to represent Warnings, and the broken wine glass found on the sides of cartons indicating that the contents are fragile.

Figure 3-4   Glyph

- *Graphs* and *charts* depict a process or a flow of information. What that information is, and how it relates to other types of information, is up to the writer. Examples include marketing graphs showing profits by years, flowcharts of a process, roadmaps of a procedure, and charts depicting the course of a project.

- *Screen captures*, also called *screen shots*, are "snapshots" of screen images; they make very effective graphics. Use them as you would any other illustration.

- *Cartoons* lend an air of informality to your document. While often used humorously, cartoons can also be sketches of activities or situations. Humor in computer documentation is a tricky technique to handle and can all too easily condescend or bore instead of amuse. Also, in a global market, documents that include one culture's humor can easily offend readers in another culture. Refer to "Illustrations and Screen Examples" in Chapter 4, "Writing for an International Audience," for more information.

Callouts

Callouts are a textual element of a drawing that clarify the illustration and provide readers with additional information or instructions. They alert readers to specific details of a drawing and conceptually connect the drawing to the text it illustrates, as shown in Figure 3-5.

Callouts are part of the drawing, so keep them in mind when placing artwork in the grid.

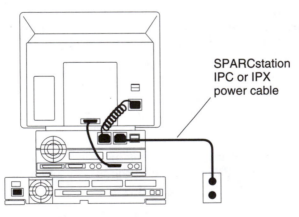

SPARCstation
IPC or IPX
power cable

Figure 3-5   Typical Callout

Writing Callouts

Because some on-line document viewers cannot display callouts that are not part of the document, callouts often need to be created within the graphic itself and then imported into the document.

When you write the text for callouts, keep the terms and descriptions simple, concise, and consistent. Address only the elements of a drawing you are discussing in the related text. For clarity, a rule of thumb for standard callout size is no greater than 1.75 inches wide and 4 lines deep, as shown in Figure 3-6.

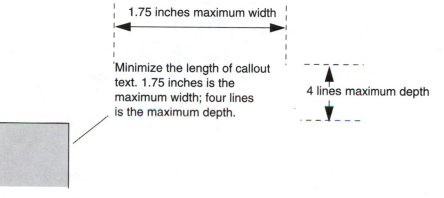

Figure 3-6   Callout Length

If your callout is longer than this, try rewriting it, breaking the information into more than one callout, or putting the information into a note or legend.

Common styles of callouts include:

- Tag-style callouts
- Sentence-style callouts
- Legends and notes
- Headings

Tag-Style Callouts

The most frequently used callouts are *tag-style callouts*. This callout style begins with a capital letter, followed by all lowercase letters. Use appropriate capitals for industry-standard acronyms and names of products. Figure 3-7 shows examples of typical callouts with and without acronyms.

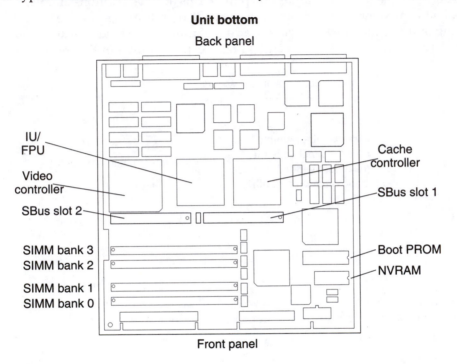

Figure 3-7   Tag-Style Callouts

Sentence-Style Callouts

Sentence-style callouts are callouts in the form of full sentences—note that they end with a period. Keep these callouts short and simple. Remember that translated sentences can be much longer than the original, so leave extra room in order to keep the callout from interfering with the drawing. See Figure 3-8 for an example of sentence-style callouts.

Use this style for:

- Descriptions of functions ("This mounting plate secures the front and back panels of the system unit.")

- Instructions ("Hook the mounting plate into the slots on the back panel of the system unit.")

- Clarifications ("Mounting plate slots are not to scale.")

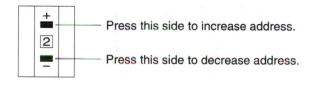

Figure 3-8   Sentence-Style Callouts

3

Legends and Notes

Legends and *notes* have the same specifications as tag-style callouts. Position legends and notes approximately 0.25 inches below the drawing, when possible, as done in Figure 3-9.

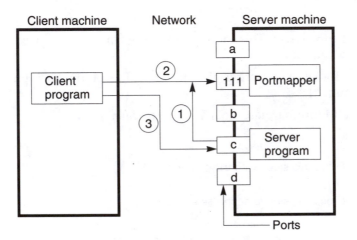

Legend: 1. Server registers with portmapper.
2. Client gets server's port from portmapper.
3. Client calls server.

Note: Multiple servers work similarly.

Figure 3-9   Legend and Note Callouts

Headings

Use *headings* to title objects or groups of objects, and to show sequential events, such as instructions or data progressions. Headings do not have leader lines.

To show sequences, label the steps alphabetically, as shown in Figure 3-10. Use capital letters and a right parenthesis, followed by the description.

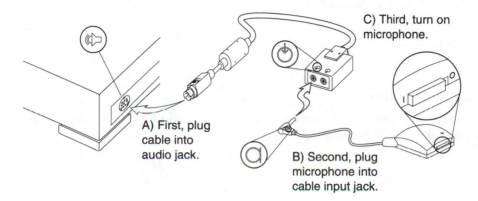

Figure 3-10   Heading Callouts

If you're not showing a sequence, you can place headings beneath the object they describe, as shown in Figure 3-11.

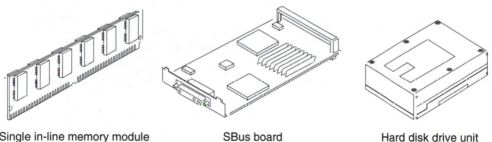

Single in-line memory module (SIMM)   SBus board   Hard disk drive unit

Figure 3-11   Heading Callouts Used as Titles

3

Aligning Callouts

Callout alignment refers to how callouts line up with each other, whether vertically, on an angle, or in an arc. *Type alignment* describes how lines of text align vertically.

Line up selected callouts either vertically or horizontally. There are three general methods of aligning callout text:

- Flush left
- Center stack
- Flush right

Flush-Left Alignment

Flush left is the most common method of aligning callout type. Figure 3-12 is a good example of the uniform look of a set of callouts aligned flush left.

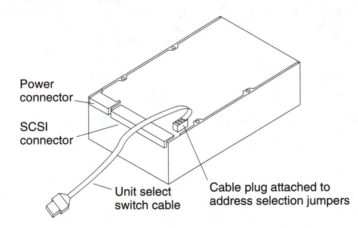

Figure 3-12   Flush-Left Callout Alignment

Center-Stack Alignment

Use center-stack callouts when centering the callout text to an object or line. Always use center-stack callouts when they are placed in a box in a flowchart or graph, on a dimension line, or centered above or below an object. Figure 3-13 provides examples.

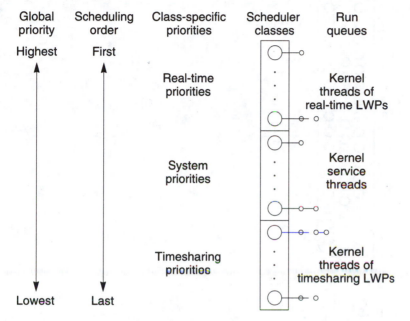

Figure 3-13   Center-Stack Callout Alignment

Flush-Right Alignment

Align callouts flush right when aligning the decimal in numeric columns.
Figure 3-14 provides an example of a flush-right column.

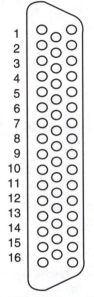

Figure 3-14   Flush-Right Callout Alignment

Arranging Callouts

Whenever possible, place callouts outside the object. Arrange callouts vertically, horizontally, diagonally, along a curve, or in a circle.

You can also use drawn objects as a visual guide to arrange callouts around a drawing. Using either the Rectangle or the Oval tool in your drawing program, draw an object around your illustration with a reasonable margin, and align your callouts to the exterior of that shape. Delete the guide when you are finished.

When you arrange callouts in an illustration, you need to consider:

- Placement around the illustration
- Block outs
- Spacing
- Sequential callouts

Callout Placement Around Illustrations

Figure 3-15 shows various callout placements you can use to arrange callouts around drawings. Placement of callouts depends upon the number of callouts, the shape of the drawing, and the location of the objects to be called out. Use the overall shape of your drawing as your guide for choosing which arrangement to use. You can use more than one arrangement in a drawing, but keep the number of leader line angles to a minimum. Try to keep the spaces between the callouts in a single drawing consistent.

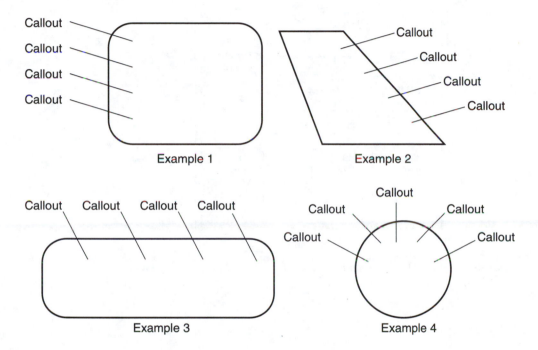

Figure 3-15   Various Callout Placements

Block Outs

Block outs are used to prevent lines in the drawing from touching any part of the callout. Block outs are centered in the object they describe. For example, when callouts are placed over 2-D objects in hardware drawings, you may have to block out underlying lines, as done in Figure 3-16.

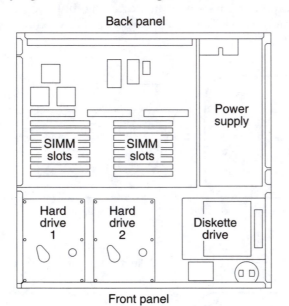

Figure 3-16   Block Out Placement of Callouts

Spacing

Place callouts far enough apart to be read clearly, and space them evenly so that a drawing does not look cluttered and is not difficult to read. Figure 3-17 shows an example of good callout spacing.

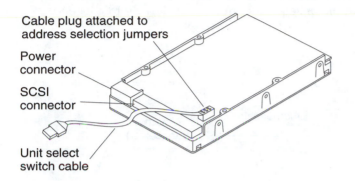

Cable plug attached to
address selection jumpers

Power
connector

SCSI
connector

Unit select
switch cable

Figure 3-17   Spacing Callouts

Sequential Callouts

When callouts are sequentially labeled, place them clockwise on the page beginning approximately at the one o'clock position. This convention is often used with internal parts breakdown (IPB) drawings when many parts are enumerated. Sequential labels can be listed numerically or alphabetically. Figure 3-18 shows an example of sequential numbers referring to a legend.

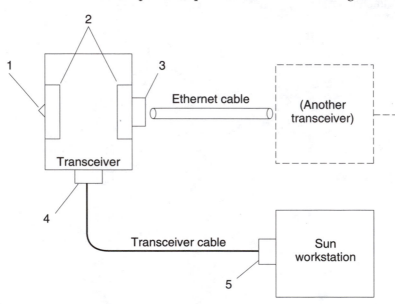

Key	Description
1	Continuing cable or terminator
2	Female N connector to transceiver or "vampire" tap cable channel
3	Male N connector to transceiver or "vampire" tap cable channel entrance
4	Ethernet transceiver D connector
5	Sun workstation to Ethernet D connector

Figure 3-18   Sequential Callouts

Avoiding Callout Taboos

There are two main callout taboos:

- *Rotated type* – Type at an angle
- *Reversed type* – White type on a black background

The best guidelines are these: If you can't read it easily, don't use it. If your eye blinks over it, don't use it.

There are occasions when you may have to break a rule. For example, if you need to show a label on a machine and the label is rotated, rotated type would be appropriate. Showing the machine rotated sideways is a much less appealing solution.

Leader Lines

Leader lines, also called *leaders*, are used to refer callouts to specific parts of a drawing. This section discusses when and how to use leaders, and how to create and place them.

Inserting Leaders

Insert leaders consistently within a drawing. In Figure 3-19, the callout "Circle" could have been placed inside the object, but for consistency it was placed outside with the other callouts. When in doubt, place callouts outside the object. If your document will be translated, place callouts outside the object whenever possible.

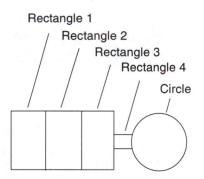

Figure 3-19   Consistent Use of Leaders

3

There are some instances when leaders are not needed.

Do not use leaders when labeling objects or actions, as shown in Figure 3-20.

SCSI workstation cable

SCSI terminator

Blank cartridge tape
(150-Mbyte tape drive)

Cleaning cartridge
(8-mm tape drive)

90/130-VAC power cord

Figure 3-20   Callouts Without Leaders

Do not use leaders in illustrations depicting a general idea or task, or with groupings of objects, as shown in Figure 3-21.

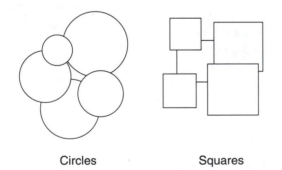

Circles   Squares

Figure 3-21   Groups of Objects Without Leaders

Read Me First!

Determining Leader Length

Leaders should be at least 1/4 inch long and spaced between 1/16 and 1/32 inch from the callout. You don't have to measure exactly; a close estimate is good enough. If you have several callouts in a single illustration, try to make the spacing consistent.

If you're having trouble visually connecting the callout with the object it explains, it's too far away; move it closer. If your object is lost in a lot of detail (for example, you want to show one wire among many), you can have the leader line touch the object, but don't have it touch text. If you're having trouble visually connecting the callout text and the leader line, they're too far apart.

Do not use long leader lines except when you have to align many callouts for appearance. Try to find an alternative to long leader lines, as shown in Figure 3-22.

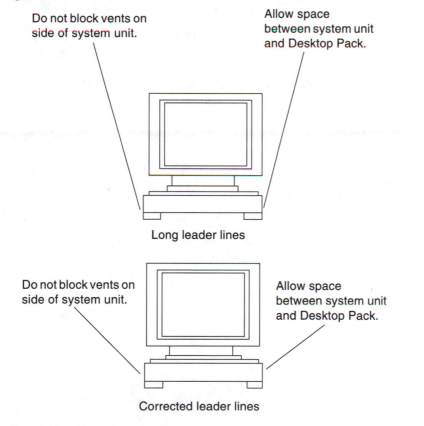

Figure 3-22   Fixing Long Leaders

Aligning Leaders and Callouts

The leader meets the closest corner of the callout or is centered with one of the callout's sides. Figure 3-23 shows the imaginary rectangle surrounding the text block.

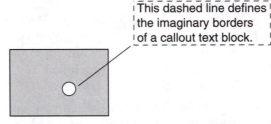

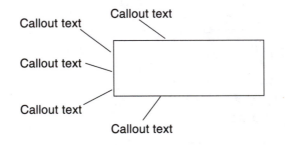

Figure 3-23   Leader Length and Placement

In general, align leaders to the corners or centers of callout sides, as done in Figure 3-24.

Figure 3-24   Aligning Leaders to Callouts

Leader Angles

To maintain balance and consistency, repeat one or two angles only, or radiate lines (see "Radiated Leaders" on page 44). If this conflicts with the specifications for callout placement, give first consideration to placement of callouts. Figure 3-25 uses repeated angles with leaders and still retains order in the placement of the callouts.

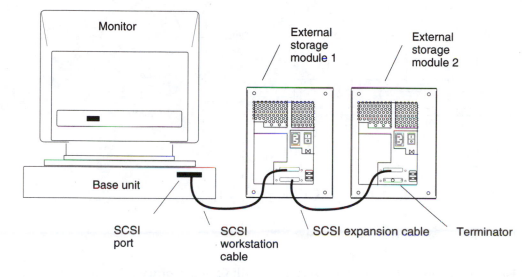

Figure 3-25   Correct Use of Leader Angles

3

Horizontal and Vertical Leaders

Avoid horizontal and vertical leaders in hardware drawings, where they could easily be mistaken for part of the object itself. Figure 3-26 shows some examples of appropriate use of horizontal and vertical leaders.

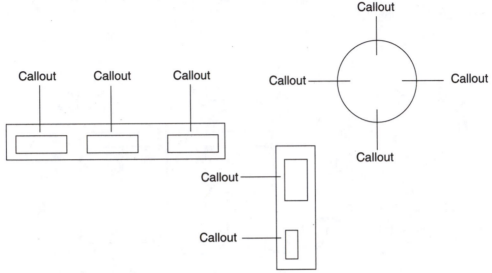

Figure 3-26   Horizontal and Vertical Leaders

Horizontal and vertical leaders work well with screen captures; they are typically placed to the left of the graphic, as in Figure 3-27.

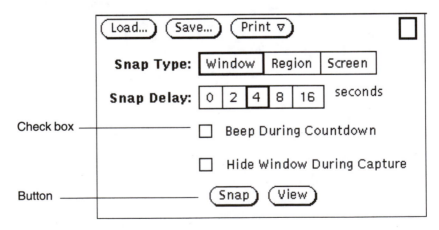

Figure 3-27   Horizontal Leaders With Screen Capture

Read Me First!

Dogleg Leaders

Dogleg leaders are leaders with a bend in them. They are often used with screen captures.

Draw leaders horizontally or vertically, with a 45-degree bend, as shown in Figure 3-28. When possible, keep callouts aligned left and placed to the left of the screen capture. Dogleg leaders are useful in crowded drawings, and are helpful in keeping callouts aligned flush left. Use them sparingly and don't use them to crowd too many callouts to one side.

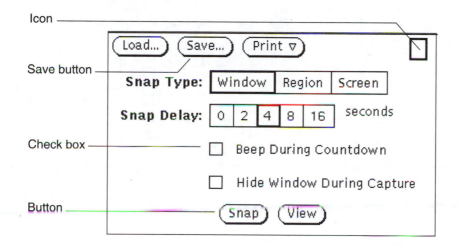

Figure 3-28   Dogleg Leaders With Screen Capture

Multiple Leaders

Use multiple leaders when you have one callout that applies to several objects, functions, commands, or contrasts. Figure 3-29 shows examples of correct use of multiple leaders. Use multiple leaders only where they add visual consistency to your illustration, and don't use more than two or three per drawing. When the objects are far apart, use another callout rather than multiple leaders.

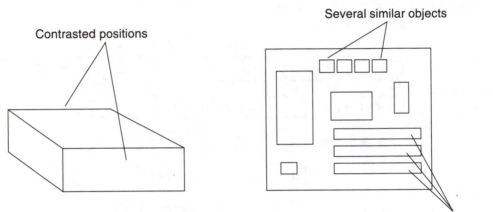

Figure 3-29   Correct Use of Multiple Leaders

Do not use multiple leaders to group dissimilar objects or groups of objects. For a group of many similar objects, a leader line to all of them is not necessary.

Figure 3-30 shows examples of incorrect use of multiple leaders.

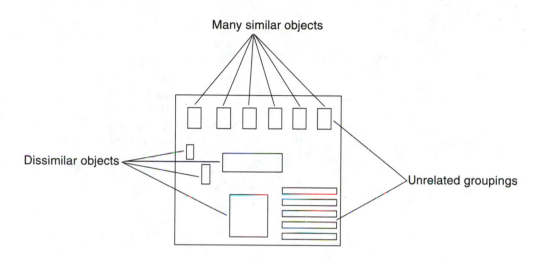

Figure 3-30   Incorrect Use of Multiple Leaders

Radiated Leaders

Figure 3-31 shows leaders that are rather long, but they were drawn that way to retain order in the placement of the callouts. The leaders are "radiated" from the drawing to enable a reader to distinguish among them more easily than among repeated angles.

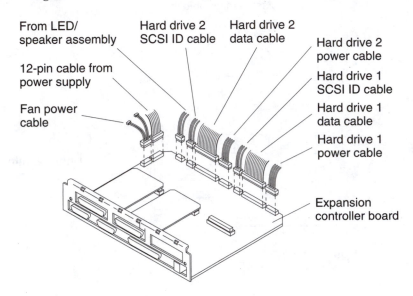

Figure 3-31   *Radiated Leaders for Orderly Callouts*

Avoiding Leader Taboos

Two common problems with leaders are crossed leaders and crossed lines.

- *Crossed leaders* – Leaders should never cross each other. Figure 3-32 illustrates an alternative to crossing leaders in a hardware drawing.

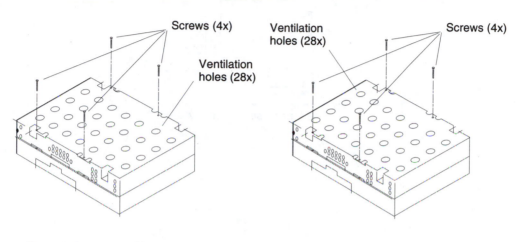

Correct placement of leaders   Crossing leaders

Figure 3-32   Crossing Leaders in Illustrations

- *Crossed lines* – Cross as few lines as possible when placing a leader. Figure 3-33 shows how a slight shift in position can mean the difference between a crossing leader and one that is more effectively placed.

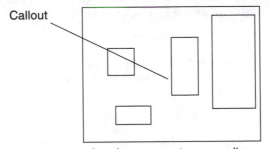

Leader crosses too many lines

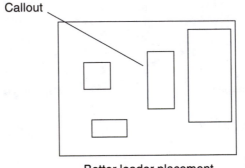

Better leader placement

Figure 3-33   Crossing Lines in Illustrations

Writing for an International Audience

4 ≡

Writing documentation that can be easily translated into other languages and delivered to audiences in other countries is becoming a mandate for the computer industry. Fortunately, the guidelines that you need to follow when writing for an international audience also apply to good technical writing in general, and can help you avoid producing documentation that is inadvertently confusing or offensive.

Internationalization involves creating a "generic" document that can be used in many cultures or easily translated into many languages. *Localization* involves converting a document that is specific to a particular language or culture into one that is specific to a different language or culture.

Working closely with translators and localization experts who are based in the countries to which you are exporting is important. See "Internationalization and Localization" in Appendix A, "Recommended Reading," for books on developing software and preparing documentation for the international market. See "Internationalization and Localization" in Appendix B, "Developing a Publications Department," for management issues related to the global market.

This chapter discusses:

- Cultural and geographic sensitivity
- Illustrations and screen examples
- Defining and using terms
- Grammar and word usage
- Numbers and symbols

≡ 4

Cultural and Geographic Sensitivity

Writers need to think globally. Conventions that are taken for granted in the United States may be handled differently in other countries. Keep in mind the following guidelines when writing for an international audience.

- Avoid using examples that are culturally bound, such as names of places that are unrecognizable to people living in other countries.

- If you do use examples that are culturally bound, use examples that represent a variety of cultures.

- Avoid political or religious references.

- Be aware that dates are displayed differently in different countries.

  - *Month, day, year* – Used mainly in the United States

  - *Day, month, year* – Used in Europe

  - *Year, month, day* – Used in Asia; also, the International Organization for Standardization (ISO) standard for numeric representation of dates

  For clarity, write out dates. For example, write "6/28/95" as "June 28, 1995." If abbreviations are necessary, define and use them consistently.

- Be aware that times are displayed differently in different countries.

  Time formats using a 12-hour clock and the ante meridiem, post meridiem system (a.m. and p.m.) may not be universally understood. Consider using a 24-hour system. For example, you might write "1:00 p.m." as "13:00."

- Always include complete information for the country in an address.

  Include telephone area codes and time zones when you provide phone numbers and calling hours in a document that may be distributed internationally. Consider the applicability of contact information. Will readers more likely write, send email, fax, or call?

- In location examples, use cities that are instantly recognizable without the state or country (for example, San Francisco, Tokyo, Paris).

- Avoid humor—it does not translate.

  What may be funny in American English, whether an illustration or written text, may be obscene in another language. Humor is strictly cultural, and it cannot be translated easily from one language to another.

- Avoid irony—even native speakers of English have difficulty discerning irony in writing.

- Avoid idioms and adages—they may be misunderstood or mistranslated.

- Don't refer to holidays.

Illustrations and Screen Examples

Follow these pointers to maximize the international appeal and comprehensibility of illustrations and screen examples.

- Use graphics instead of text wherever possible to illustrate a complex concept. Write text so that it complements the message conveyed by a graphic.

- Use graphics liberally. However, not everyone reads from left to right, so you should indicate the intended sequence in which a reader needs to refer to the graphics.

- Use graphics that are internationally acceptable.

  For example, almost every country has its own type of power plug. Instead of illustrating each type of plug, use generic plugs and receptacles, as in Figure 4-1.

  However, when describing various types of plugs and receptacles, illustrate and label the type used in each country, as shown in Figure 4-2.

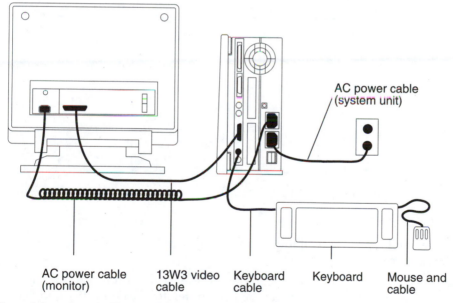

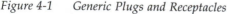

AC power cable (monitor)   13W3 video cable   Keyboard cable   Keyboard   Mouse and cable

Figure 4-1   Generic Plugs and Receptacles

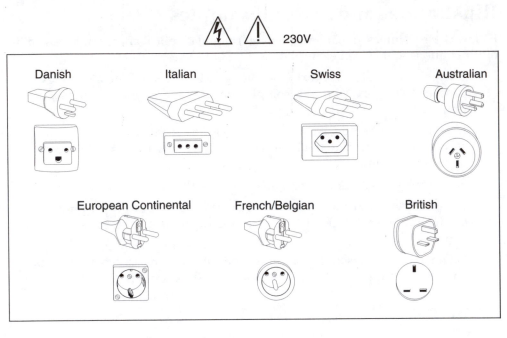

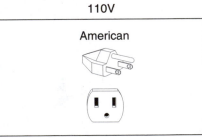

Figure 4-2   International Plugs and Receptacles

- Leave ample space for callout text in graphics, as translated text may require more space than English text.
- Make certain that the callouts correlate to the paragraph text. Use callouts instead of text if the concept can be best understood graphically and needs little explanation.
- Use charts and tables to clarify essential information; they are internationally recognized by readers as containing important material.
- Format callouts so that you can edit them separately from the graphic.

- Do not use a hand in a *symbolic* gesture. Just about any way you position a hand can be considered an obscene gesture, depending upon the culture, as illustrated in Figure 4-3.

Figure 4-3   *Possible Obscene Gestures*

- When using screen snapshots or screen examples, make sure that the machine names, login names, and system names are not culturally offensive.

Instead of:

```
%purgatory
```

Use a generic example:

```
%machine_name
```

- Avoid using road signs in graphics, as they differ from country to country.
- Avoid references to alcohol or alcohol-related material, as this could be offensive.
- Be careful when using everyday objects in examples. Make sure that the object exists in most countries, and keep in mind that it may be interpreted in various ways in different parts of the world.

   For example, a light bulb may be used to indicate light, but not the concept of an idea.

- Avoid using trendy objects, historical references, or film, cartoon, or other video characters.
- Avoid using animals, as they may carry symbolic significance.
- Consider the aesthetics of color and typography for different cultures.

≡ 4

Definitions and Use of Terms

Follow these guidelines to avoid common pitfalls that make translators and readers uncertain of your intended meaning.

- Use general or nontechnical terms consistently. Provide translators with a glossary and a style sheet.

- Define new terms and technical terms that do not appear in a regular dictionary the first time they appear in your text. Italicize terms when first defining them. Also include these terms in a glossary.

- Avoid jargon or slang.

  If a word does not appear in a standard dictionary or a technical source book, or if a term is specific to your company, but is not defined in the text or in your glossary, do not use it. If translators cannot look up an unfamiliar word, they may have to guess at its meaning.

- Avoid using abbreviations (such as "cont.," "incl.," and "attachmnt.").

  Many languages do not have abbreviations and cannot accommodate them. Define abbreviations and acronyms the first time you use them in text, and provide a list of them at the end of the book as part of the glossary, in an appendix, or in a separate list of abbreviations. When you define the term, give the spelled-out version first, followed by the acronym or abbreviation in parentheses.

  See "Abbreviations and Acronyms in Text" in Chapter 7, "Technical Abbreviations, Acronyms, and Units of Measurement," for more information about using abbreviations and acronyms.

- Use all terms consistently throughout a document.

  Synonymous words in a document can be troublesome for a translator. Although to you "show," "display," and "appear" may seem similar enough to use interchangeably, a translator may think you used different words deliberately for different meanings and may interpret the text incorrectly.

- Avoid using general modifiers that could be interpreted in several ways.

  For example, there is no Japanese equivalent for the word "nice." The Japanese translator has to choose which Japanese word gives the closest meaning to the word "nice." The choices include "smart," "pretty," "cute," "good," and "useful." If you wrote "the nice display" (meaning "the useful display"), it could be translated as "the cute display," changing the intent of the sentence.

Grammar and Word Usage

Follow these guidelines for grammar and word usage to ensure that your document can be accurately and easily translated.

- Try to keep sentences clear and short (under 25 words). A long, complicated sentence that contains several ideas or concepts is difficult to translate and to understand.

- Make sure that your spelling and usage are correct. Use electronic spelling checkers and copy editors to ensure accuracy.

- Don't leave out articles, such as "the," "a," and "an."

  Good: Place a screwdriver in the groove.

  Poor: Place screwdriver in groove.

- Be careful about using the same word in multiple grammatical categories, such as verb, noun, and adjective.

  Good: Place the file in a folder.

  Poor: File the file in a file folder.

  Using "file" as a verb, noun, and adjective is confusing to translators, who may have to use a different word in each case. This is an extreme example, but try not to use the same term in different ways. Also, do not use several terms to refer to the same thing.

- Be precise about using the terms "when" and "if." Use "when" only when the event is inevitable. Use "if" when the event is conditional.

  "*When* the prompt appears" implies that the prompt will appear.

  "*If* the prompt appears" implies that the event may or may not occur.

- Make sure that you distinguish between restrictive and nonrestrictive clauses.

  Consider the differences in meaning for the following two sentences:

  > Note the ready light that appears on the front panel. (restrictive)

  > Note the ready light, which appears on the front panel. (nonrestrictive)

  In the first sentence, the reader is told to note the ready light on the front panel—not the one on the side panel or back panel, but the one specifically on the front panel.

  In the second sentence, the reader is told merely to note the ready light; the sentence also states that the light happens to be on the front panel, implying that there is no other ready light anywhere else. The minor difference in meaning could confuse translators or non-native speakers of English.

- Avoid ambiguous phrases.

  For example, "first-come, first-served" is ambiguous. If possible, rewrite as "in the order received" or "in the order in which they are received."

- Avoid vague and uncertain references between a pronoun and its antecedent. Make sure that the noun to which a pronoun refers is clear.

  Unclear: When the results were announced by the researchers, they were questioned by the other experts in the field.

  Does "they" refer to the results or to the researchers? For clarity, rewriting the sentence is often necessary (especially to avoid repeating the noun).

  Awkward: When the results were announced by the researchers, the results were questioned by other experts in the field.

  Better: Other experts in the field questioned the results announced by the researchers.

Numbers and Symbols

Most of the world uses the metric system, although many people in the United States are familiar only with the U.S. equivalents for the metric system. Also, number and currency formats vary worldwide. For example, in many countries commas and decimal points are used differently. As a courtesy to readers who use different numeric systems, consider the following:

- When providing U.S. measurements, include the metric equivalent in parentheses if it is appropriate for the product you are writing about. Most standard English dictionaries contain a U.S.-to-metric conversion chart under the "metric" entry.

- Avoid using the # symbol to indicate "pound," a single quote (') to indicate "foot," and double quotes (") to indicate "inch."

  These symbols are not recognized in many countries outside of the United States. Each measurement should include its metric system equivalent when appropriate.

- If you use the word "billion" or "trillion," explain the term in a footnote so that the exact value will be known to readers in all countries.

  For example, "One billion equals 10^9" or "One trillion equals 10^{12}."

Such footnotes are necessary because the words "billion" and "trillion" (and larger denominations) have different meanings in different countries. In the United States, 1 billion means 1,000,000,000 (10^9); in some other countries, it means 1,000,000,000,000 (10^{12}). For more information about the international use of numbers, refer to "Table of Numbers" in *Merriam-Webster's Collegiate Dictionary,* 10th ed. (Merriam-Webster, Inc., 1995).

- Avoid using symbols such as "/" and "&" in text.

Many symbols have multiple meanings, and translators may have difficulty deciding which meaning you intended. For example, the "/" symbol can mean "and," "or," "and/or," "with," "divide by," "root," or "path-name divider."

- Be aware that numerals may carry certain connotations.

For example, in some Asian countries "4" indicates "death" and "9" signifies "suffering." Other numbers with connotations are "13," "69," and "666."

≡ *4*

Read Me First!

Legal Guidelines 5 ≡

Technical publications professionals need to follow legal guidelines that cover the proper usage and marking of trademarks and the protection of intellectual property. Trademarks and materials that can be copyrighted are among a company's most valuable assets. Everyone who is involved in the preparation of materials that use trademarks or who creates materials subject to copyright has a responsibility for securing and protecting the copyrights and trademarks.

This chapter contains information about:

- Copyrights
- Trademarks
- Protecting proprietary documents and electronic communication

Note – This chapter sometimes advises you to check with the legal department in your company. If you do not have a legal department, check with counsel specializing in trademark and copyright law.

Copyrights

Copyright is a type of legal protection, actually a set of distinct rights, granted by federal law for most literary, musical, dramatic, and other types of intellectual works, including computer programs. A 1978 law established a single system of protection for all published and unpublished "original works of authorship fixed in any tangible medium of expression from which they can be perceived, reproduced or otherwise communicated." With limited exceptions, no one may copy or reproduce, display, prepare derivative works, or distribute copies to the public by sale, rental, lease, lending, or other transfer of ownership of copyrighted works without permission of the copyright owner.

Copyrights do not protect the ideas and concepts contained in a work, but only the expression of such ideas and concepts. For this reason, copyright is not always the best single means of protection for materials containing valuable information that may be exploited. Confidential business information is usually best protected as a trade secret. It should also include a proprietary label (see "Proprietary Information" on page 64) and should not be disclosed to third parties.

What Should You Copyright?

The following types of materials intended for external distribution should contain a copyright notice:

- Publications—books, articles, research papers, and brochures
- Advertising copy
- Photographs
- Catalogs
- On-line documents (including pages on the World Wide Web)
- Product labels
- Product documentation
- Software applications
- Source and object code for software products

Check with your legal department if you don't know whether you should copyright a particular type of work.

Copyrighting Your Work

Note – This section and the one that follows, "Registering Your Copyright," necessarily discuss copyright law in the United States. If you are in a different country, check your local requirements.

Work is considered *created* both in part and in entirety when it is prepared over a reasonable period of time and *fixed* in a copy by the author for the first time. At this stage, the work is sufficiently stable that it can be communicated to and understood by others. For example, a chapter that you write becomes protected by copyright law the moment you save it to a disk file. Copyright protection is *automatically* granted under federal law for work created and published after March 1, 1989. However, affixing a copyright notice to each copy of a published work is an important step in preserving the copyright. For this reason, works suitable for copyright protection should always contain a proper copyright notice.

A copyright notice comprises:

- The symbol © or the word "Copyright"
- The year of first publication of the work
- The name of the owner of the copyright

Your legal department may have approved specific copyright statements. The copyright portion of these statements should not be modified (except for the date) without consulting your legal department.

An example of a copyright statement follows:

© 1995 Kaytram, Inc., 2550 Regis Avenue, Mountain View, California 94043-1100 U.S.A.

All rights reserved. This product and related documentation are protected by copyright and are distributed under licenses restricting their use, copying, distribution, and decompilation. No part of this product or related documentation may be reproduced in any form by any means without prior written authorization of Kaytram, Inc., and its licensors, if any.

Copyrights for Revised Documents

A previously copyrighted document that is recast, transformed, or adapted is considered a *derivative work* for purposes of copyright. For example, your manual would be considered a derivative work if you added a new section, chapter, or appendix. On the other hand, your manual would *not* be considered a derivative work if you merely fixed some spelling or style errors, changed the order of the chapters, or applied new templates.

If your document is a derivative work, you need to change the date in the copyright notice to the date that applies to the created derivative work. You also may need to include the earlier dates in a copyright notice for a derivative work. Check with counsel.

If your document is not a derivative work, use only the original copyright date. Do not change the copyright date or add other dates to it.

Duration of Copyright Protection

Copyrights, unlike trademarks or patents, subsist from the time a work is created. Copyrights exist for a finite number of years, generally the life of the author plus 50 years or, if done as a work made for hire for an employer, for 75 years from the date of publication, after which time the work becomes part of the public domain.

Copyright Ownership

Generally speaking, if materials are written by an employee in the course of his or her job, the employer is the owner of the copyright. For example, if you were a technical writer who wrote software installation guides for Spacely Software, Spacely would own the copyright. If you wrote short stories on your lunch hour, *you* would retain the copyright.

Copyrights in works created by independent contractors are owned by the independent contractors. However, this ownership is usually transferred to the employer if the contractor has signed a standard Personal Services Agreement or otherwise assigned his or her rights to the employer in writing. Departments that use independent contractors should make sure that one of these assignment documents exists for each contractor.

In some situations, especially when you are marketing software products licensed by third parties, the copyright may be held by someone else. Check with your legal department if you have questions about copyright ownership.

Registering Your Copyright

To take full advantage of the legal protection afforded a copyrighted work, you may also have to register the work with the United States Copyright Office. Registration is a relatively straightforward process: It requires completing a one-page application and including either a copy of the work or, in the case of software, a portion of the source code (usually the first and last 25 pages with portions blocked out to protect trade secret information) as *deposit* or other *identifying material.*

Registration is almost always a prerequisite for:

- Filing an infringement action
- Obtaining statutory damages (so that the party whose work has been infringed does not have to prove economic loss to recover damages)
- Obtaining attorney's fees
- Enlisting the U.S. Customs Service to bar the importation of illegal copies of the registered work

A federally registered copyright also gives the registrant various procedural advantages should it elect to take action against an infringer. There is no universal international copyright protection, but works copyrighted in the United States may be protected in foreign countries under various treaties and conventions.

Trademarks

A *trademark* is a word, phrase, name, symbol, logo—or a combination of these elements—adopted and used by a company to identify its particular *brand* of products and services, and to distinguish them from those of other companies.

A *trade name* is the name of a company or its abbreviation under which business activity is conducted. Do not place a ™ (for trademark) or ® (for registered trademark) symbol after a trade name. Some names, though, may be used in either category. For example, Sun is the trade name of a company (Sun Microsystems, Inc.), but Sun™ is also the trademark for that company's line of products. Whether to use the ™ designation depends upon the particular reference being made.

A *service mark* is the same as a trademark except that it distinguishes and identifies the source of a service rather than a product. Service marks usually appear in advertising for the service. Use a superscripted SM symbol for service marks.

Types of Trademarks

Trademarks fall into two major categories:

- Trademarks that are registered with the U.S. Patent and Trademark Office or the trademark offices of other countries
- Trademarks that are claimed by a company but have not been registered

Both types of trademarks are protectable. Registered trademarks, however, are subject to stronger enforcement measures and may be required in certain countries to prevent other parties from "pirating" your trademarks (which, in some cases, could mean disruption of shipments of your products).

Proper Use of Trademarks

The scope and strength of a company's exclusive rights to its trademarks may be weakened if they are not used properly, even if they are registered. A number of well-known names—such as "escalator," "aspirin," and "cellophane"—were once trademarks, but those names have fallen into such common use that they now may be used by anyone.

All of your company trademarks should have:

- The appropriate notice (® or ™) the first time the trademark is mentioned in the text
- The appropriate legend (often found at the end of the brochure or on the back of the title page) attributing the trademarks to your company

After the first proper designation, use the trademark name as a proper adjective, without the ® or ™ symbol.

To protect trademarks:

- Use ® with registered trademarks. Don't use this mark with unregistered trademarks or when a registration certificate has not yet been received.

- For unregistered trademarks, use only the ™ designation. Do not add a trademark symbol when referring to trade names (the name under which a company does business).

  If you are in doubt about which symbol to use, ask your legal department.

- Designate trademarks on book covers and the first time they are mentioned in text (this includes chapters, appendixes, and the preface). Most publications do not put trademark symbols in the table of contents, chapter or appendix titles, section heads, tables, or captions.

- Except as noted, *always* use trademarks as proper adjectives.

  Don't use trademarks as nouns. Trademarks are proper adjectives and should always be used with the common noun that they modify (for example, "PowerPC™ microprocessor," "FrameMaker® software," and "OpenWindows™ environment").

  There is one exception often made to this rule. If the trademark itself includes some sort of descriptive or generic component, and thus creates a redundancy in writing, the trademark may be used by some companies as a singular noun. "PacerPrint®" and "ClickArt®" are examples of trademarked product names that might fall under this rule, so you wouldn't have to continually write "PacerPrint printer" and "ClickArt art."

- Never use trademarks in the possessive or the plural.

  Form the possessive or plural from the common noun that the trademark describes (see "Common Nouns Used With Trademarks").

  Wrong: My dog ate the Macintosh's microphone.
  Right: My dog ate the Macintosh computer's microphone.

  Wrong: UNIX is fun and easy to learn.
  Right: The UNIX system is fun and easy to learn.

  Wrong: Turn off your Selectric.
  Right: Turn off your Selectric typewriter.

- Do not capitalize common nouns preceded by proper adjectives. If the noun is part of a product name, capitalize it as you would a proper noun.

- Never parenthetically define existing acronyms or abbreviations that are trademarked terms.

Common Nouns Used With Trademarks

Trademarks are proper adjectives. As such, they modify nouns. The term *common noun* (sometimes called *generic noun*) refers to the noun that a trademark describes. Always link a trademark with an appropriate common noun. Do not capitalize the common noun.

Under some circumstances, certain trademarks may be used as singular nouns. See "Proper Use of Trademarks" for more information.

Here are some examples of frequently used common nouns in the computer industry:

application	interface	screen
architecture	kernel	server
client/server systems	machine	software
distributed computing solution	operating environment	system
environment	operating system	system software
equipment	package	technology
features	peripheral	tool
files	platform	unit
graphical user interface (GUI)	printer	window environment
hardware	program	workstation

Using common nouns in place of trademarks can be effective, but make sure that the reader is clear about the product to which you are referring. For example, in many cases "operating system" is a useful replacement for "SunOS™ 5.x system software." However, if you are comparing the SunOS 5.x software with another operating system, this will not work. In such cases, continue to include the trademarked product name with the common noun. Similarly, be careful using such words as "application" or "toolkit" by themselves.

If you use a common noun, define it and then use it consistently. Repeat the definition after each major head if it will help readers who are retrieving the information on line. If the context of the reference is obvious to the reader, you do not need to repeat the common noun's definition too often.

5

Proper Use of Third-Party Trademarks

Treat *third-party trademarks* (trademarks from other companies) with the same respect as trademarks from your company—as proper adjectives with the correct ® or ™ notices—and give them appropriate attribution as trademarks.

- Mark third-party trademarks with the correct ® or ™ notice on book covers and the first time they appear in text (this includes chapters, appendixes, and the preface). Most publications do not put trademark symbols in the table of contents, chapter or appendix titles, section heads, tables, or captions.

- Make an effort to consult product or marketing groups, or the third parties themselves, to make sure that third-party trademarks are given appropriate attributions. When such a consultation is not reasonably practical, mark the third-party product name with a ™ and include a general attribution similar to the following in the trademark legend after the specific attributions:

   All other product names mentioned herein are the trademarks of their respective owners.

- In running text, do not put two trademarked terms belonging to different companies next to each other unless there is a license or agreement between the two parties. For example, you would not write "Sun Ada" unless a licensing agreement existed between Sun Microsystems, Inc., and the U.S. Department of Defense.

- Never parenthetically define existing acronyms or abbreviations that are trademarked terms.

Proprietary Information

Proprietary information is defined broadly as any information that gives your company a competitive advantage or could be damaging to your company if the disclosure of this information is out of your company's control.

Proprietary information includes:

- Drafts of manuals, research papers, and product notes
- Technical data
  - Object code
  - Source code
  - Flowcharts
  - Schematics

- Detailed information about new products before public announcement
  - Project code names and descriptions
  - Product features (processing speed, graphics capability)
  - Target dates for production
  - Pricing
  - Market placement and strategies, and customer information
  - Costs and other financial information
  - Bugs
  - Design data
  - Diagnostic and reliability data
- Email messages
- Presentation materials (including handouts, transparencies, and slides)
- Employee information, such as performance reviews and salary information

Protecting Proprietary Documents

Proprietary documents need to be protected by appropriate labeling from the time they are created until they are released or are safely destroyed. This section lists and explains three commonly used proprietary labels, which often appear in boldface type.

- *Company Name* **Proprietary: Internal Use Only**

  Use this label for general information, such as job listings that are distributed throughout the company.

- *Company Name* **Proprietary/Confidential: Need-to-Know**

  Use this label for all pre-release product documentation and information. This covers all information that is distributed to product teams (manuals, release notes, research papers, or specifications).

- *Company Name* **Proprietary/Confidential: Registered**

  Use this label for highly sensitive information, where numbered copies are made and carefully controlled.

In general, most documentation should have the label "*Company Name* Proprietary/Confidential: Need-to-Know." Be sure to remove the proprietary label before producing the final production version of the documentation.

If you have any questions about proprietary labels, send them to counsel in your legal department.

5

Protecting Electronic Communication

Email has become the quickest way to communicate in the computer industry. However, email writers must be as careful to protect proprietary information in these messages as they are to protect hard-copy documents.

Any email containing proprietary information should include an appropriate label in the email header, such as:

- *Company Name* Proprietary: Internal Use Only
- *Company Name* Proprietary/Confidential: Need-to-Know

Confirm the names on an email alias before sending information to a large audience, and create smaller aliases for particularly sensitive topics. Don't distribute messages beyond the alias or to addresses outside of your company.

Mechanics of Writing 6≡

Error-free writing entails more than using good grammar. You must also use correct mechanics of writing in your documents. The *mechanics of writing* specify how words should be used when printed, whereas *grammar* reflects the form of words and their relationships within a sentence. For instance, if you put a sentence-ending period outside of quotation marks ("You have to stop".) you have made an error in the mechanics of writing, not grammar. An enjoyable book that discusses differences between mechanics and grammar is *Dr. Grammar's Writes From Wrongs,* by Richard Francis Tracz (Vintage Books, A Division of Random House, Inc., 1991).

The mechanics of writing guidelines in this chapter work well for computer documentation, but other style guides may suggest different rules that are equally effective. It doesn't matter which rules you follow as long as you are consistent within your document or documentation set. See Chapter 8, "Constructing Text," for other options you can use.

This chapter discusses:

- Capitalization
- Contractions
- Numbers and numerals
- Punctuation
- Usage of common computer terms

Capitalization

Writers tend to err on the side of too much capitalization. The chief reason to capitalize a word is that it is *proper*—not because the word has greater status than other words. A *proper noun* identifies a specific member of a class, whereas a *common noun* denotes either the whole class or any random member of the class. For example, King Henry VIII (a particular member of a class) was a king of England (the class itself).

Use an industry-accepted dictionary or other resource to verify capitalization of computer terms. Refer to "Reference Books" in Appendix A, "Recommended Reading," for a list of suggested resources.

When to Capitalize

This question may help you determine whether a noun is proper or common:

> Does an article or another limiting word (such as "a," "the," "this," "some," or "certain") appear before the noun in question?

If so, it is probably a common noun.

Note the difference between the following sentences:

> Use a text editor to change the information in your file.

> Use Text Editor to change the information in your file.

In the first sentence, the article "a" makes it clear that the writer is pointing to no particular member of the group of text editors. Therefore, "text editor" is a common noun. But in the second sentence, the absence of an article or limiting word helps make it clear that the writer is pointing to only one member of the group. In that case, capitalize the proper noun "Text Editor."

In general, capitalize:

- The letters of many abbreviations and acronyms
- The first letter of entries in unnumbered (bulleted) lists
- The first letter of the first term used in figure callouts and proper nouns in figure callouts
- The first letter of "table," "figure," "appendix," "chapter," and "section," when followed by a letter or number

  > Turn to Chapter 3.

  > Turn to the next chapter.

- The first letter of the names of function keys on a keyboard

  > Control key   Escape key

- The first letter of the first word in a sentence, unless the sentence begins with a literal command name or other literal computer term that is not capitalized (try to write in a way that avoids such occurrences)

  > Use the `format` utility to divide the disk into slices.

  > `format` enables you to divide the disk into slices.

- The first word of a complete sentence following a colon

    The software saves time: You can now press a single key to accomplish what used to take hours of complex calculations.

    Select from two options: Save stores your changes, and Discard erases your changes.

- The first letter of any word in a title or head, with the exception of conjunctions and articles, prepositions of fewer than four characters, and the "to" in infinitives, unless they appear at the beginning or end of the title or head

    See Chapter 3, "Using the Mouse."

- The second element of a hyphenated compound in a title or head, only if it is a noun or proper adjective, or if it has equal force with the first element

    Installing a Half-Inch Disk Drive

    Ordering Third-Party Peripherals

    Using a Look-up Table

- Figure and table captions, using the same rules you establish for titles and heads in your document

When Not to Capitalize

In general, do *not* capitalize:

- The word "page" or "step" when followed by a number

    Refer to page 45.

    Skip step 3 if you are not installing a CD-ROM drive.

- The first letter of the words in certain phrases, even though the phrases ordinarily appear in a shortened form in capital letters

    field-replaceable unit   FRU

    direct memory access   DMA

- Any word for the sole reason of emphasizing it (use italics for emphasis)
- Variable names used in code examples
- Alphanumeric keys in a key combination

    Control-q   Escape-m

- Words in figure callouts other than the first word or proper nouns

- In a title or head, conjunctions, articles, prepositions of fewer than four characters, and the "to" in infinitives, unless they appear at the beginning or end of the title

  Elements of the User Interface

  Using the Numeric Keypad to Enter Data

  Saving Time With ACME Software

Contractions

You can't write naturally without using contractions, but:

- Don't overuse them.
- Avoid obscure contractions and nonstandard usages and regionalisms.

  mustn't   mightn't   shan't

  "ain't" and "don't" to mean "does not"

- Never create your own contractions.
- Use "it's" correctly. "It's" is the contraction of "it is." "Its" is the possessive of "it."

  It's the correct contraction to use.

  Its features are many.

- Likewise, use "you're" correctly. "You're" is the contraction of "you are." "Your" is a possessive adjective.

  You're looking at the data entry window.

  Check the settings on your modem.

Numbers and Numerals

A *number* is a characteristic that describes a unit within a collection. A number is expressed by *numerals* (1, 2, 3, 4) or by words. *Cardinal numbers* use words such as "one, two, three," while *ordinal numbers* use words such as "first, second, third."

In computer documentation, you will most often use numerals when numbers are discussed in text.

Spelling Out Numbers

Spell out:

- Numbers from zero through nine, unless the number is part of a measurement

    three computers (a count)   3 inches (a measurement)

- Approximations

    You can choose from hundreds of applications for your computer.

- Extreme values, such as "million" and "billion," but precede them with a numeral

    3 million instructions per second

- Any number that begins a sentence

    Ten files are required.

- The first number if a numeral immediately follows the number

    Print twelve 500,000-byte files.

Using Numerals

Use numerals for:

- Numbers 10 or greater
- Numbers less than 10 if they are of the same type and appear in the same paragraph as numbers of 10 or greater

    The menu offers 11 options, but you will use only 4.

- Negative numbers
- Most fractions
- All percentages
- All decimals, including the leading zero

    0.15   1.25

- All measurements

    6 pounds   3.5-inch disk drive

- Chapter, section, part, page, figure, and table numbers

    Part 4   Chapter 6

Punctuating Numbers and Numerals

Numbers and numerals generally require the same punctuation as words. Punctuating numbers and numerals becomes troublesome, however, when they are compounded.

- Do not hyphenate numbers or numerals when they serve as single modifiers.

    Your file comprises 500,000 bytes.

- Hyphenate numbers or numerals in compound modifiers.

    Print your 500,000-byte file.

- Do not use a comma in numerals of four digits.

    1028   6000

- Use a comma in numerals of more than four digits.

    10,000   600,000

Using Fractions

The usage of numerals for fractions depends upon the context. Sometimes spelling out the fraction or using decimals is the preferred form.

- Use numerals for fractions in tables and for units of measurement, but spell out common fractions in running text.

    1/2-inch tape drive

    half the users in the test

- Use a space between a numeral and its related fraction.

    8 1/2 inches

- If a fraction is being used as a modifier, insert a hyphen between the fraction and what it is modifying.

    8 1/2-inch width

- Use decimals when that is the industry standard.

    5.25-inch drive

    3.5-inch diskette

    1/2-inch tape drive

- Spell out a numeric modifier of a fraction.

    ten 1/2-inch tape drives (10 tape drives for 1/2-inch tape)

    10 1/2-inch tape drive (tape drive for 10 1/2-inch tape)

Punctuation

This section reviews basic punctuation rules and guidelines for the English language, and notes exceptions that are specific to computer documentation.

Note – Traditional punctuation marks take on specialized meanings in the context of programming languages. A classic example is that of quotation marks in the C shell or Bourne shell, which provide specialized, non-intuitive meanings for single quotes ('), double quotes ("), and back quotes ('). Watch for these in your writing and editing.

Apostrophe

Use an apostrophe:

- **In contractions.** Apostrophes replace omitted letters in contractions.

    can't   aren't   it's   you're

- **In place of numerals.** Apostrophes also replace omitted numerals.

    Class of '66   Spirit of '76

- **For possessives.** Use apostrophes to note the possessive case of nouns.

    If they do not end in "s," add an apostrophe and an "s" to most indefinite pronouns, singular nouns (including collective nouns), and plural nouns.

    the file's properties   someone's system

    the group's privileges   women's rights

    To form the possessive of singular nouns ending in "s" (or its sound), you often add an apostrophe and an "s."

    the mouse's buttons   the bus's capacity

    When the addition of an "s" produces an awkward sound, add only the apostrophe.

    ACME Systems' employees

    In a few cases, however, either is acceptable.

    M. Travis's files   M. Travis' files

    Add an apostrophe to form the possessive of plural nouns that end in "s."

    the Travises' files   the boards' interrupts

    Add an apostrophe and an "s" to the last word of the compound to form the possessive of most compound constructions.

    each other's files   anyone else's business

The possessive of two or more proper nouns depends upon ownership. In the first example, ownership is joint; in the second, individual.

Malcolm and Mary's files   Malcolm's and Mary's files

- **To form plurals.** Use an apostrophe to form the plurals of most numerals and symbols, lowercase letters, or single uppercase letters.

drive B's   ~'s and #'s   −f's

The plural possessive of single lowercase letters and single uppercase letters will be awkward in the plural possessive form. A rewrite often can avoid this situation.

The dots on the "i's."   The "i's'" dots.

The apostrophe is not necessary (although not incorrect) when you are forming the plural of two or more unitary uppercase letters or numerals.

plug in all CPUs   the operating system of the 1990s

Brackets

Brackets are not substitutes for parentheses. To preserve brackets' unique service as meaningful signals to readers of computer documentation, construct sentences in a way that minimizes the grammatical need for such punctuation.

Use brackets:

- **With parenthetic text.** Use brackets when inserting a parenthetic word or phrase into material already enclosed by parentheses.

It often makes sense to place comments within a menu file (see page 154 of *Advanced Skills*, Revision A [May, 1991] for more information).

- **In optional command-line entries.** Brackets can set off an optional part of a command line.

date [*yymmddhhmm*]

Colon

Use a colon:

- **To introduce a list.** A colon helps introduce a list or a series. See "Lists" in Chapter 8, "Constructing Text," for other guidelines to use when punctuating lists.

  Note that the colon takes the place of introductory phrases such as "as follows" and "listed below."

  > Default settings include four secondary groups: `operator`, `devices`, `accounts`, and `networks`.

  > Three options available from the Diagnostics menu are:
  > - Test computer
  > - Inspect computer
  > - Upgrade firmware

  When the introduction to a list or steps in a procedure is a complete sentence, use of the colon is optional. However, judge whether the ensuing list seems to flow naturally from the introduction; in effect, to "complete" the introductory sentence. If so, use a colon.

  > Learn how to send a message by following these steps:

  > To send a message:

  > Follow the steps in the next exercise to learn how to mail a message.

- **Before explanatory text.** A colon indicates that the initial clause will be further explained or illustrated by information that follows the colon.

  The colon serves as a substitute for phrases such as "in other words," "namely," or "for instance."

  Notice in the following example that the first word following the colon is capitalized. Capitalize the statement if it is a complete sentence; don't capitalize it if it's a fragment.

  > It was a software package doomed from the start: Its price was $12,000, its language written in ALGOL, and its documentation was printed on 300 sheets of unbound paper.

- **After an introduction.** A colon appears after an introduction to a long, "formal" statement or question.

  > Here is the choice: Do you want to save the file or delete it?

  > Remember this cardinal rule: Never reboot your system until you've saved all of your files.

6

Comma

Use a comma:

- **In a series.** Commas separate the items in a series of three or more words, phrases, and clauses.

  > Among your hidden files are `.cshrc`, `.defaults`, `.login`, `.logout`, and `.mailrc`.

  Use a comma before the conjunction that joins the last two items of a series.

  In complex sentences, however, elimination of the final serial comma sometimes helps to separate a long series from an independent clause.

  > Before going to the next step, position the pointer on the desktop, display the menu, make your selection and confirm the result, and you will ensure the accuracy of your data.

  However, if an independent clause already contains a comma, use a semicolon to separate items in a series.

  > The window has a menu bar, which lists available menus; a palette, which shows graphics tools; and a working area, where you draw.

- **To separate parts of a sentence.** Commas break long sentences into comprehensible parts.

  A comma separates independent clauses joined by the coordinating conjunctions "and," "but," "yet," "for," "nor," and "or." Place the comma before the conjunction.

  > You don't have to back up your files, but doing so is prudent.

  > She lost all of her work, yet she still doesn't back up files.

  Omit the comma between two short independent clauses in a sentence.

  > Back up your work or you're fired.

  > Display the menu and choose Save.

  Use a comma to separate a subordinate clause or long introductory phrase from the rest of the sentence.

  > Using the text editor, change the last line of the file.

  > By recording transactions and automating billing, the financial software saves time and prevents costly errors.

  Use a comma after a dependent adverbial clause that starts a sentence, but not if the clause appears in normal order in the sentence.

  > Because this feature automatically updates system files, it saves time.

  > This feature saves time because it automatically updates system files.

Read Me First!

A comma separates an introductory modifier from the rest of the sentence.

> Hopefully, he entered the personnel office.

> Confident she had saved her work, she logged out.

A comma sets off introductory interjections or transitional words.

> Oh, did you need more information?

> Fine, go ahead and set up that meeting.

- **With nonrestrictive phrases.** Use a comma to set off nonrestrictive clauses or phrases.

  > The mail icon, which looks like a mailbox, flashes.

  > Writers often refer to this book, which is a style guide for the computer industry.

- **With parenthetic text.** A comma sets off parenthetic material that is not enclosed by parentheses.

  > The software, with its simple interface, will decrease input time by 50 percent.

- **In addresses.** Use a comma to set off components of an address when the address is linear within a sentence.

  > Write to ACME Systems, Santa Maria, California.

- **With appositives.** In most cases, use commas instead of dashes to set off a single appositive.

  > The monitor, hardware that looks like a television set, has only one function.

- **In dates.** A comma separates components of a date. The comma is optional, however, when there are only two components of the date.

  > She was hired on January 1, 1989, and left six months later.

  > :She was hired in January 1989.

Dash (Em Dash)

Use an em dash, with *no space* before or after the dash:

- **With an appositive series.** Use an em dash before and after an appositive series.

  Three vital pieces of hardware—the keyboard, the system unit, and the monitor—are packed in the largest carton.

  Use of dashes in the example above avoids the confusion that could be caused by using commas both within the series and to set off the series from the rest of the sentence.

  In most cases, use commas instead of dashes to set off a single appositive.

  The monitor, hardware that looks like a television set, sits on top of the system unit.

- **To show abrupt changes.** An em dash shows an abrupt change in thought or sentence construction.

  Log in to the system—but that's an obvious first step.

- **For emphasis.** Use an em dash to set off material for emphasis.

  Become superuser—you must type su to do this—and delete all files in M. Travis's directory.

  All of the options—Create, Modify, and Save—enable you to customize the software's features.

Dash (En Dash)

Use an en dash:

- **To indicate a range.** Use an en dash, without surrounding spaces, to indicate a range, such as pages in a book.

  Refer to pages 16–24.

- **To indicate negative numbers.** An en dash can serve as the minus sign for numbers that are less than zero. However, a hyphen is also an acceptable way to depict a minus sign.

  Do not operate this equipment in temperatures lower than –10 °C.

- **In lists.** In an unnumbered (bulleted) list, you can use an en dash to separate an introductory word or phrase from its explanation. When you use this list format, put a space before and after the en dash.

  The word processing software features:

  - *Automatic save* – Saves changes every two minutes
  - *Automatic backup* – Creates a backup file when you exit
  - *Automatic recall* – Tracks the last 20 transactions

Ellipsis Mark

An ellipsis mark comprises three ellipsis points (periods) with a space between each point. A space separates the ellipsis mark from preceding and subsequent text and punctuation.

Use an ellipsis mark:

- **For omissions.** An ellipsis mark shows that something has been omitted from a sentence, phrase, or clause.

  When the system displays, "Do you want the . . . settings now?"

  Add a period when a complete sentence ends with an ellipsis mark or when you have omitted entire sentences from quoted matter. In effect, you type four periods, each preceded by a space.

  You see this message on the screen: "If you like, you may press the Stop key . . . ."

  The system then displays this message: "This system is being configured . . . . When this system is configured, it will finish booting."

- **For pauses.** Use an ellipsis mark to indicate a pause when quoting a displayed message.

  Reformatting page. Wait . . .

Hyphen

Because the computer industry has developed unique terminology, the use of hyphens has become troublesome. Computer documents are often littered with unnecessary hyphens. Refer to Table 6-1 for a list of words and phrases that have come into general acceptance as hyphenated, unhyphenated, or compound.

If you can't find a specific word or term in the table, apply this general rule: Hyphenate a multiword expression when used as a modifier; do not hyphenate the expression when used as a verb or noun.

the check-in procedure	check in the material
the direct-access password	if you have direct access
the end-user application	writing for end users

This section includes guidelines for when *to use* a hyphen and when *not to use* a hyphen.

Use a hyphen:

- **With compound modifiers.** With some exceptions, use a hyphen to form a compound modifier when the modifier is used before the noun. Use hyphens with numerals in compound modifiers, as well.

    This applies only to user-defined functions.

    Print your 500,000-byte file.

Hyphenate a compound modifier when it appears *before* the noun. Usually, when it appears *after* the noun, a compound modifier should not be hyphenated.

    An easy-to-remember mail alias is a person's first initial and last name.

    A mail alias that is easy to remember is a person's first initial and last name.

Occasionally, the initial elements of two or more compound modifiers within the same sentence share the same final element. In these constructions, hyphenate the initial elements, even when they are not joined directly to the final, common element.

    The sending application and the receiving application expect 8- and 7-bit characters, respectively.

    These computers have file-, directory-, and labor-saving features.

- **To prevent ambiguity.** Hyphens clarify ambiguous text.

    "Ed owns a toy-repair store" vs. "Ed owns a toy repair store"

    "He recovered the disc" vs. "He re-covered the disc"

- **With prefixes and suffixes.** A hyphen often is used between a prefix or suffix and a root word when the combination results in double letters. However, use the guidelines found in a standard dictionary for some terms.

re-enable	co-organizer	shell-like
reentry	unnumbered	misspell

Use a hyphen to join numbers and *proper* nouns or adjectives with the following prefixes. (These same prefixes, however, are usually joined without hyphens to common nouns and modifiers.)

anti-	mid-	neo-	non-
pan-	pro-	un-	

Almost without exception, hyphens join the following prefixes with the main word of a compound.

all-	ex-	self-

- **In fractions.** A hyphen separates the components of a spelled-out fraction.

    The resulting `core` file will take up nearly one-third of your system memory.

- **In key combinations.** Use a hyphen to separate key combinations.

    Press Control-Shift-q.

Do not use a hyphen:

- **For industry-accepted terms.** Do not hyphenate compound words that have come into general acceptance as single words.

    backup   database

- **To construct verbs.** Do not hyphenate two words that are used as a verb, but that are hyphenated when used as a compound modifier.

    Dial up only after reading the dial-up instructions.

    Look up the value in the look-up table.

- **With a compound modifier (adverb) ending in "ly."** Never hyphenate a compound modifier that includes an adverb ending in "ly."

    An easily remembered mail alias is a person's first initial and last name.

- **With numerals as single modifiers.** Do not hyphenate numerals or numbers when they serve as single modifiers.

    Your file comprises 500,000 bytes.

- **With some prefixes and suffixes.** Do not use a hyphen in a word that is listed as unhyphenated in a standard dictionary and that uses a common prefix.

bi	inter	meta	micro	mini	multi
non	pre	post	un	under	

- **To indicate a range.** Use an en dash instead of a hyphen to indicate a range. Do not put a space either before or after the dash.

    Refer to pages 16–24.

Table 6-1   *Hyphenation Guidelines*

Word or Phrase	Usage
A	
add on	verb
add-on	noun, modifier
all-inclusive	modifier
alphanumeric	modifier
analog-to-digital	modifier
antiglare	modifier
automount	verb
autotransformer	noun
B	
back panel	noun
back-panel	modifier
backplane	modifier, noun
backquote	modifier, noun
backslash	modifier, noun
backspace	modifier, noun, verb
back up	verb
backup	modifier, noun
bandwidth	modifier, noun
benchmark	modifier, noun
bidirectional	modifier
bisynchronous	modifier
bitmap	modifier, noun
bitstring	modifier, noun
breakpoint	modifier, noun
build in	verb
built-in	modifier
C	
card cage	noun
CD-ROM	noun, modifier

Table 6-1   Hyphenation Guidelines (Continued)

Word or Phrase	Usage
check in	verb
check-in	noun, modifier
checklist	noun
check out	verb
check-out	noun, modifier
client-server	modifier
coaxial	modifier
code name	noun
colormap	modifier, noun
command line	noun
command-line	modifier
compact disc	noun
coprocessor	modifier, noun
coroutine	modifier, noun
cross-refer	verb
cross-reference	noun
cross-section	noun
cross-sectional	modifier
D	
database	modifier, noun
datasheet	modifier, noun
datastream	modifier, noun
daughterboard	modifier, noun
debug	modifier, noun, verb
deselect	verb
desktop	modifier, noun
dial up	verb
dial-up	modifier
digital-to-analog	modifier
direct access	noun
direct-access	modifier

Table 6-1   *Hyphenation Guidelines (Continued)*

Word or Phrase	Usage
directory name	noun
double click	noun
double-click	modifier, verb
download	verb
downtime	modifier, noun
drag and drop	noun
drag-and-drop	modifier
dual-access	modifier
dual-density	modifier
dump file	noun
E	
electromagnetic	modifier
email	modifier, noun
endpoint	noun
end user	noun
end-user	modifier
entry level	noun
entry-level	modifier
F	
feedback	noun
file name	noun
file server	noun
file sharing	noun
file-sharing	modifier
file system	noun
firmware	noun
fixed length	noun
fixed-length	modifier
fixed point	noun
fixed-point	modifier
floating point	noun

Read Me First!

Table 6-1   Hyphenation Guidelines (Continued)

Word or Phrase	Usage
floating-point	modifier
flowchart	modifier, noun
follow up	verb
follow-up	modifier
frame buffer	noun
front end	noun
front-end	modifier
front panel	noun
front-panel	modifier
full height	noun
full-height	modifier
G	
general-purpose	modifier
grayscale	modifier, noun
H	
half-height	modifier
hard copy	noun
hard-copy	modifier
hardwire	verb
hardwired	modifier
hexadecimal	modifier
high end	noun
high-end	modifier
high level	noun
high-level	modifier
high performance	noun
high-performance	modifier
high resolution	noun
high-resolution	modifier
high speed	noun
high-speed	modifier

Table 6-1   *Hyphenation Guidelines (Continued)*

Word or Phrase	Usage
host name	noun
host-name	modifier
hot key	noun
hotline	modifier, noun
I	
in-line	modifier
inode	noun
interconnect	modifier, noun, verb
interface	modifier, noun
internetwork	modifier, noun
interoperability	noun
interprocess	modifier, noun
K	
keyboard	modifier, noun
keymap	modifier, noun
keypad	modifier, noun
keyword	modifier, noun
L	
laser disc	noun
left-justified	modifier
list file	noun
local-area	modifier
lock up	verb
lockup	modifier, noun
log file	noun
log in	verb
login	modifier, noun
log out	verb
logout	modifier, noun
look up	verb
look-up	modifier

Table 6-1   Hyphenation Guidelines (Continued)

Word or Phrase	Usage
low end	noun
low-end	modifier
low level	noun
low-level	modifier
low resolution	noun
low-resolution	modifier
lowercase	modifier, noun
M	
mailbox	noun
mainframe	modifier, noun
mass storage	noun
mass-storage	modifier
metadisk	modifier, noun
metafile	modifier, noun
microcode	modifier, noun
microprocessor	modifier, noun
microsecond	noun
midrange	modifier, noun
minicomputer	modifier, noun
miniroot	noun
monochrome	modifier
motherboard	modifier, noun
multilevel	modifier
multimedia	modifier, noun
multiplexer	modifier, noun
multiprocessor	noun
multitasking	modifier
multitrack	modifier, noun
multiuser	modifier
N	
newline	modifier, noun

Table 6-1   *Hyphenation Guidelines (Continued)*

Word or Phrase	Usage
node name	noun
noninterlaced	modifier
nonproprietary	modifier
nontechnical	modifier
nonzero	modifier
O	
object-oriented	modifier
off line	adverb
off-line	modifier
off-load	verb
on-board	modifier
on line (or online)	adverb
on-line (or online)	modifier
P	
path name	noun
path-name	modifier
pop-up	modifier
print out	verb
printout	modifier, noun
pull-down	modifier
pull-right	modifier
R	
random access	modifier
raster file	noun
raster-file	modifier
read-only	modifier
real time	noun
real-time	modifier
re-create	verb
restart	verb
retry	verb

Read Me First!

Table 6-1   Hyphenation Guidelines (Continued)

Word or Phrase	Usage
right-justified	modifier
runtime	modifier, noun
S	
SBus	noun
scrollbar	noun
self-test	modifier, noun
set up	verb
setup	modifier, noun
shut down	verb
shutdown	modifier
single-tasking	modifier
source code	noun
source-code	modifier
source file	noun
source-file	modifier
standalone	modifier
start up	verb
startup	modifier, noun
subdirectory	noun
subentry	noun
subroutine	modifier, noun
subset	modifier, noun
subsystem	modifier, noun
subtest	noun
superblock	noun
supercomputer	modifier, noun
superuser	noun
T	
2-D	modifier
3-D	modifier
text-only	modifier

Table 6-1   Hyphenation Guidelines (Continued)

Word or Phrase	Usage
time-out	modifier
timesharing	modifier, noun
timestamp	noun
time zone	noun
token ring	modifier
toolkit	modifier, noun
tradeoff	noun
triple-height	modifier
troubleshoot	verb
troubleshooting	modifier
U	
upload	modifier, verb
uppercase	modifier, noun
uptime	noun
user ID	noun
user name	noun
V	
video disc	noun
W	
wide-area	modifier
wildcard	modifier, noun
word processing	modifier
workgroup	modifier, noun
worksheet	noun
workspace	modifier, noun
workstation	noun
write-back	modifier
write-enable	verb
write-enabled	modifier
write-protect	verb

Table 6-1   *Hyphenation Guidelines (Continued)*

Word or Phrase	Usage
write-protected	modifier
Z	
Z-buffer	noun

Parentheses

Before using parentheses, consider whether the parenthetic material is, in fact, important enough to be included at all. If it is, perhaps the text fits better without parentheses within the paragraph. If the information is not important, don't write it.

Use parentheses:

- **With digressive text.** Use parentheses to enclose *relevant* material that should not be part of the main sentence, either because it would be confusing if punctuated otherwise or because it is digressive.

    The Font menu, which provides four options (Regular, Italic, Bold, Bold Italic), is easy to use.

    You can save these settings in a "quick-start" file (explained fully in the next step) to load them automatically.

- **For elaboration.** Parentheses enclose material that further explains an element of the main sentence, but is not critical to the sentence's meaning.

    To suppress the printing of address information (particularly useful for messages with many addresses), remove the check from the Print Header box.

- **In lists.** Use can use either two parentheses or one parenthesis to offset letters or numerals that designate items listed within a sentence.

    Choose from (a) keyboard entry, (b) mouse entry, and (c) voice entry.

    Choose from (a keyboard entry, (b mouse entry, and (c voice entry.

- **With first occurrences.** Parentheses enclose special keyboard symbols, and abbreviations and acronyms when they first appear in text.

    The operating system inserts a tilde (~) when a file name is too long.

    The software package tracks maintenance on your heating, ventilating, and air conditioning (HVAC) systems.

6

- **To enclose an entire sentence.** Use parentheses to enclose an entire sentence that is relevant to information presented in the paragraph, yet dispensable to the paragraph's meaning. When an entire sentence is enclosed in parentheses, place the final parenthesis after the sentence's final punctuation mark.

Whole paragraphs should never be parenthetic.

> Position the pointer on the top scrollbox and click the left mouse button. (For detailed instructions on scrolling windows, see page 33.)

Period

Use a period:

- **In file and directory names.** A period is sometimes part of a file name (separating a file name from a file extension).

> The procedures are in the `howto.doc` file.

> The `ls -a` command lists `.cshrc` and `.orgrc` among your hidden files.

In the UNIX system, a period also serves as an abbreviation for the current directory.

> To copy a file into the current directory, type `cp ~/work/budget .`

- **To end a sentence.** Use a period to end a declarative or imperative sentence.

> Computer documentation is always grammatically precise.

Whenever possible, avoid ending a sentence with a verbatim command that the must be typed. A reader might misinterpret the sentence's ending punctuation as an integral part of the command.

> "Type `boot` to restart the computer." vs.
> "To restart the computer, type `boot`."

- **With abbreviations.** A period follows some common abbreviations. Refer to Table 7-1 in Chapter 7, "Technical Abbreviations, Acronyms, and Units of Measurement."

> The meeting is at 10 a.m. on Friday.

Read Me First!

Quotation Marks

Use quotation marks:

- **For quotes.** Quotation marks indicate that material—other than literal computer commands, system messages, file names, and so forth—was taken verbatim from another source.

  Don't enclose verbatim commands, system messages, file names, and so forth in quotation marks. In some cases a reader may be misled into thinking that the quotation marks are an integral part of what is to be typed.

  > The comment in the `.login` file states that the file is "read in when you exit from the login shell."

- **Around chapter titles.** Use quotation marks to enclose titles of chapters in a book.

  > For more information about editing mail, see Chapter 5, "Sending and Receiving Mail."

- **For highlighting.** Quotation marks highlight a word or phrase when it is used in an uncommon way, or when it is itself the subject of discussion.

  > You can use the `tee` command to take a "snapshot" of your keystrokes.

  > The word "menu" is often used in technical writing.

- **Around single letters.** Quotation marks also surround single letters.

  > The letter "x" denotes . . . .

No single rule governs the placement of quotation marks that are next to other punctuation marks. Whether the final quotation mark follows or precedes another punctuation mark depends upon context.

- Place the final quotation mark *after most* adjacent punctuation marks, no matter how long or short the quoted material is.

  > "Yes," he replied, the program is written.

- Always place the final quotation mark *before* a colon or semicolon.

  > There are three buttons on your "mouse": left, middle, and right.

  > Some of your files are "hidden"; that is, their names do not appear in a standard `ls` directory listing.

- Place the final quotation mark *after* a question mark or an exclamation point when the question or exclamation is part of the quoted material.

  The system prompts, "Do you want to continue?"

  The user guide answers the question, "What does it do?"

  But place the final quotation mark *before* a question mark or exclamation point that is not part of the quoted material.

  How do I display a list of files that are "hidden"?

Semicolon

Use a semicolon:

- **Before explanatory statements.** Use a semicolon before a phrase that introduces an explanatory or summarizing statement.

  The Open key is a toggle key; that is, a key with alternating functions.

  Some of the options are not available; for example, the Undo option is grayed out and the Spell option is not displayed.

- **With independent clauses.** Use a semicolon to separate independent clauses joined by conjunctive adverbs, such as "hence," "however," or "therefore."

  Because this software is supplied in source-code form, users may adapt it for use on other systems; however, modified source code is not supported by ACME Systems.

  A semicolon also separates independent clauses not joined by a conjunction.

  Don't write the introduction; all introductions are now written by Marketing.

- **In a series.** A semicolon separates items in a series when the items themselves include commas.

  The Reply button provides the following options: Reply (all), include; Reply, include; Reply (all); and Reply.

Usage of Common Terms in Computer Documentation

The computer industry has created new terms, given new meanings to existing terms, and established capitalization, punctuation, spelling, and syntax guidelines for terms. Table 6-2 lists some troublesome computer terminology and provides usage guidelines for these terms. Also refer to Table 7-1 in Chapter 7.

Table 6-2   Usage Guidelines

Word or Phrase	Usage
Allen wrench	Note capitalization.
appendixes	Do not use "appendices."
baud rate	Often incorrectly assumed to indicate the number of bits per second (bps) transmitted, baud rate actually measures the number of events, or signal changes, that occur in one second. In most instances when "baud rate" is used, the correct term is "bps." (For example, a so-called 9600-baud modem actually operates at 2400 baud, but it transmits 9600 bits per second, and thus should correctly be called a 9600-bps modem.) Check your source material before using the term "baud rate."
Boolean	Note capitalization.
CD-ROM	Use to refer generically to CD-ROM media; for example, "The software comes on CD-ROM discs." If referring to a specific compact disc for installation or other purposes, "CD" is acceptable; for example, "Put the CD into the caddy." Add the adjective "audio" if referring to CD-ROM media that contain wholly or mostly music.
CD-ROM drive	Do not say "CD drive" or "CD player." If a drive will only play audio CDs, refer to it as an "audio CD-ROM drive."
disc	Use for optical discs.
disk	Use for any disk other than an optical disc.
diskette	State the size (3.5 or 5.25 inches), and don't use the modifier "floppy."
Ethernet	Note capitalization.
indexes	Do not use "indices."
input	Use as a noun only, not as a verb.
interface	Use as a noun or modifier, not as a verb.

Table 6-2   Usage Guidelines (Continued)

Word or Phrase	Usage
internet	Use lowercase when referring to a collection of networks that function as a single large virtual network.
Internet	Use an initial capital when referring to a large internet comprising large national backbone nets and various regional and local networks worldwide. The Internet uses the Internet Protocol suite.
output	Use as a noun only, not as a verb.
Phillips screwdriver	Note capitalization and spelling.
press	Use to indicate the action of pressing a key that does not echo to the screen; the Control key is one such example.
type	Use to indicate the entering of information: "Type the following command."
UNIX	Note capitalization.

Technical Abbreviations, Acronyms, and Units of Measurement 7

Computer documentation requires extensive use of abbreviations, acronyms, and units of measurement, many of which have become generally accepted "words" in the industry language. As with any word in a sentence, it is important that you use abbreviations, acronyms, and units of measurement accurately and with consistent meaning in your documentation. To do this, rely on industry definitions for these terms; don't create your own abbreviations or acronyms. Reference books of this type include *The New IEEE Standard Dictionary of Electrical and Electronics Terms*, *IBM Dictionary of Computing*, and *Microsoft Press Computer Dictionary*.

This chapter provides guidelines for:

- Using abbreviations and acronyms
- Punctuating abbreviations and acronyms
- Abbreviating units of measurement

The chapter concludes with a table listing abbreviations and acronyms for some commonly used words, phrases, and units of measurement.

Abbreviations and Acronyms in Text

An *abbreviation* is a shortened form of a word or phrase that is used in place of the entire word or phrase. "CPU" for central processing unit, "Btu" for British thermal unit, and "SGML" for Standard Generalized Markup Language are examples of abbreviations. An *acronym* is an easily pronounceable word formed from the initial letters or major parts of a compound term. "COBOL" for common business-oriented language, "pixel" for picture element, and "ROM" for read-only memory are common acronyms.

When using abbreviations or acronyms, follow these guidelines:

- In most cases, write out the full word or phrase and enclose its abbreviation or acronym in parentheses the first time it is used. Then continue using the abbreviation or acronym alone.

  For example, a local-area network (LAN) comprises computer systems that can communicate with one another via connecting hardware and software. LANs are often used today.

- If you cite a term only once or twice in a document, don't shorten it unless the abbreviation or acronym is well known.

- If an abbreviation or acronym appears often in your document, repeat the spelled-out version in each chapter where it is used.

- Do not shorten trademarked terms or spell out trademarked terms that appear to be abbreviations or acronyms.

- When using an acronym, make sure that its pronunciation is natural and obvious to a reader.

  The acronym "SCSI," for example, is pronounced "scuzzy." A user who doesn't know that "SCSI" is pronounceable may expect to see "*an* SCSI port," not "*a* SCSI port." In such cases, provide a pronunciation key when you first use the acronym by itself, as in this example:

  > A small computer system interface (SCSI—pronounced "scuzzy") cable connects the disk drive to the SCSI port.

Punctuation of Abbreviations and Acronyms

While you usually do not have to add any punctuation to abbreviations and acronyms, a few exceptions are made.

- Use periods or other punctuation marks in abbreviations or acronyms when it is standard form.

  > in. for inch   I/O for input/output   3-D for three-dimensional

- Add an "s" and no apostrophe to form the plural of abbreviations or acronyms that contain no periods.

  > PCs   ISVs   GUIs

- Add an apostrophe and "s" to form the plural of abbreviations or acronyms that use internal periods.

  > M.S.'s   Ph.D.'s

Units of Measurement

Follow these guidelines when abbreviating units of measurement:

- Do not abbreviate common American units of measurement, such as "inches," "pounds," and "feet," unless space conservation (such as within a table column) is an overriding concern.

- Use standard abbreviations for units of measurement with great care.

  For example, the difference between Mb and MB is the difference between a megabit and a megabyte. Avoid this confusion by consistently spelling out a term like "megabyte" or by using the less-abbreviated form, "Mbyte."

- Be aware that most abbreviations for units of measurement already account for plurals.

  For example, the abbreviation for 1 kilowatt and 10 kilowatts is written the same way: kW.

- If an abbreviation for a unit of measurement consists of more than one letter, leave a space between the numeral and the abbreviation, but if an abbreviation consists of only one letter, do not leave a space.

      12 mm   12V

- Include the metric or U.S. equivalent of a unit of measurement, when appropriate.

      1 in. (2.54 cm)   1m (3.2808 ft)

≡ 7

List of Abbreviations and Acronyms

Countless abbreviations and acronyms are used in the computer industry. Table 7-1 lists some of the common ones.

Note – This list is not intended to be comprehensive. While it includes some common terms, other resources, such as those mentioned at the beginning of this chapter, contain many more. And, of course, new abbreviations and acronyms are created as technologies emerge. Also note that definitions of terms can vary from one computer discipline to another, and even within the same discipline, the style and wording of definitions may vary slightly from source to source.

Table 7-1   Abbreviations, Acronyms, and Units of Measurement

Abbreviation	Name or Term
Numerics	
2-D	two-dimensional
3-D	three-dimensional
A	
A	ampere
amp	ampere
ABI	application binary interface
AC	alternating current
ACM	Association for Computing Machinery
A/D	analog-to-digital
ADC	analog-to-digital converter
ADDR	address
ADP	automatic data processing
ADPCM	adaptive differential pulse code modulation
ADU	automatic dialing unit
AF	audio frequency
AFC	automatic frequency control
AI	artificial intelligence
ALGOL	Algorithmic Language
ALU	arithmetic and logic unit

Table 7-1   Abbreviations, Acronyms, and Units of Measurement (Continued)

Abbreviation	Name or Term
a.m.	ante meridiem (morning)
AM	amplitude modulation
ANSI	American National Standards Institute
API	application program interface
ARPANET	Advanced Research Projects Agency Network
ASCII	American National Standard Code for Information Interchange
ASIC	application-specific integrated circuit
ASR	automatic send/receive
async	asynchronous
ATM	asynchronous transfer mode
AUI	attachment unit interface
B	
b	bit
B	byte
BASIC	beginners all-purpose symbolic instruction code
BBS	bulletin board system
BCD	binary-coded decimal
BER	bit error rate
BIOS	Basic Input/Output System
bisync	binary synchronous
BJT	bipolar junction transistor
BNF	Backus-Naur Form
BOF	beginning of file
BOT	beginning of tape
bpi	bits per inch
bps	bits per second
Bps	bytes per second
BSC	binary synchronous communication
BSD	Berkeley Software Distribution
BSD	block schematic diagram
Btu	British thermal unit

Table 7-1   Abbreviations, Acronyms, and Units of Measurement (Continued)

Abbreviation	Name or Term
C	
c	centi (prefix)
C	coulomb
C	C programming language
°C	Celsius
°C	centigrade
CAD	computer-aided design
CAE	computer-aided engineering
CAI	computer-assisted instruction
CAM	computer-aided manufacturing
CASE	computer-aided software engineering
CCD	charge-coupled device
ccw	counterclockwise
CD-ROM	compact disc read-only memory
CDE	Common Desktop Environment
CGA	color graphics adapter
CISC	complex instruction-set computer
CLUT	color look-up table
CMOS	complementary metal-oxide semiconductor
COBOL	common business-oriented language
cpi	characters per inch
CPM	Control Program for Microcomputers
cps	characters per second
CPU	central processing unit
CRC	cyclic redundancy check
CRT	cathode ray tube
CRU	customer-replaceable unit
CTCA	channel-to-channel adapter
CUI	character user interface
cw	clockwise

Table 7-1   Abbreviations, Acronyms, and Units of Measurement (Continued)

Abbreviation	Name or Term
D	
d	deci (prefix)
da	deka (prefix)
D/A	digital-to-analog
DAC	digital-to-analog converter
DAT	digital audio tape
dB	decibel
DBMS	database management system
DC	direct current
DCE	data communication equipment
DES	Data Encryption Standard
DIF	data interchange format
DIMM	dual in-line memory module
DIP	dual in-line package
DMA	direct memory access
DMM	digital multimeter
DOS	Disk Operating System
dpi	dots per inch
DRAM	dynamic random access memory
DSP	digital signal processor
DSR	data set ready
DTD	Document Type Definition
DTE	data terminal equipment
DTR	data terminal ready
DVM	digital voltmeter
E	
EAROM	electrically alterable read-only memory
EBCDIC	extended binary-coded decimal interchange code
ECC	error checking and correction
ECC	error correcting code
ECL	emitter-coupled logic

Table 7-1   Abbreviations, Acronyms, and Units of Measurement (Continued)

Abbreviation	Name or Term
EDI	electronic data interchange
EDP	electronic data processing
EEPROM	electrically erasable programmable read-only memory
EEROM	electrically erasable read-only memory
EGA	enhanced graphics adapter
EIA	Electronics Industry Association
E-IDE	Enhanced Integrated Drive Electronics
EISA	Extended Industry Standard Architecture
EMI	electromagnetic interference
EOF	end of file
EOT	end of tape
EOT	end of transmission
EPROM	erasable programmable read-only memory
EPS	Encapsulated PostScript
EPSF	Encapsulated PostScript Format
F	
F	farad
°F	Fahrenheit
FAQ	frequently asked question
FAT	file allocation table
fax	facsimile
FCB	file control block
FE	framing (bit) error
FET	field-effect transistor
FIFO	first-in, first-out
FILO	first-in, last-out
FIPS	Federal Information Processing Standard
FLOP	floating-point operation
FLOPS	floating-point operations per second
FM	frequency modulation
Fortran	formula translation

Table 7-1   Abbreviations, Acronyms, and Units of Measurement (Continued)

Abbreviation	Name or Term
FPA	floating-point accelerator
FPLA	field-programmable logic array
FPU	floating-point unit
FRU	field-replaceable unit
FTP	File Transfer Protocol
G	
g	gram
G	giga (prefix)
Gbyte, GB	gigabyte
GID	group identification
GIF	graphics interchange format
GUI	graphical user interface
H	
H	henry
HBA	host bus adapter
hex	hexadecimal
HF	high frequency
HFS	hierarchical file system
HMOS	high-speed negative-channel metal-oxide semiconductor
HSM	hierarchical storage management
HTML	Hypertext Markup Language
HTTP	Hypertext Transfer Protocol
Hz	hertz
I	
IC	integrated circuit
IDE	Integrated Drive Electronics
IEEE	Institute of Electrical and Electronics Engineers
IHV	independent hardware vendor
I/O	input/output
IOP	input/output processor
IP	Internet Protocol

Table 7-1   Abbreviations, Acronyms, and Units of Measurement (Continued)

Abbreviation	Name or Term
IPC	interprocess communication
IPS	inches per second
IPS	instructions per second
IPS	interrupts per second
IR	information retrieval
IR	infrared
IRQ	interrupt request
ISA	Industry Standard Architecture
ISA	instruction-set architecture
ISAM	indexed sequential access method
ISDN	integrated services digital network
ISO	International Organization for Standardization
ISV	independent software vendor
J	
JFET	junction field-effect transistor
JPEG	Joint Photographic Experts Group
K	
k	kilo (prefix)
°K	Kelvin
Kb	kilobit
Kbyte, KB, K	kilobyte
kg	kilogram
kHz	kilohertz
km	kilometer
KSR	keyboard send/receive
kV	kilovolt
kW	kilowatt
kWh	kilowatt-hour
L	
LAN	local-area network
lb	pound

Table 7-1   Abbreviations, Acronyms, and Units of Measurement (Continued)

Abbreviation	Name or Term
LCD	liquid crystal display
LED	light-emitting diode
LF	low frequency
LIFO	last-in, first-out
LILO	last-in, last-out
LISP	List Processor
LP	line printer
lpi	lines per inch
LSB	least significant bit
LSD	least significant digit
LSI	large-scale integration
LSN	least significant nibble
LU	logical unit
LUN	logical unit number
LUT	look-up table
M	
μA	microampere
μF	microfarad
μg	microgram
μH	microhenry
μm	micrometer
μs	microsecond
μV	microvolt
μW	microwatt
m	meter
m	micro (prefix)
m	milli (prefix)
M	mega (prefix)
mA	milliampere
MA	megampere
MAC	medium access control

Table 7-1   *Abbreviations, Acronyms, and Units of Measurement (Continued)*

Abbreviation	Name or Term
MAC	memory access controller
Mb	megabit
Mbps	one million bits per second
Mbyte, MB	megabyte
mF	millifarad
MFLOPS	millions of floating-point operations per second
mg	milligram
mH	millihenry
MHz	megahertz
MIDI	Musical Instrument Digital Interface
MIPS	million instructions per second
MIS	management information system
mm	millimeter
MNP	Microcom Networking Protocol
modem	modulator-demodulator
MOS	metal-oxide semiconductor
MOSFET	metal-oxide semiconductor field-effect transistor
MPEG	Moving Pictures Experts Group
ms	millisecond
MSB	most significant bit
MSD	most significant digit
MSI	medium-scale integration
MSN	most significant nibble
MTBF	mean time between failures
MTTR	mean time to repair
MTU	magnetic tape unit
MTU	maximum transfer unit
MUX	multiplexer
mV	millivolt
mW	milliwatt
·MW	megawatt

Read Me First!

Table 7-1   Abbreviations, Acronyms, and Units of Measurement (Continued)

Abbreviation	Name or Term
N	
n	nano (prefix)
NaN	not a number
NC	no connection
NC	normally closed
NC	numerical control
NF	noise figure
NIC	network interface card
NMOS	negative-channel metal-oxide semiconductor
NO	normally open
NRZ	nonreturn to zero
NTSC	National Television Standards Committee
NVRAM	nonvolatile random access memory
O	
Ω	ohm
OCR	optical character recognition
OEM	original equipment manufacturer
OS	operating system
OSI	Open Systems Interconnection
oz	ounce
P	
p	pico (prefix)
PABX	private automatic branch exchange
PAL	programmable array logic
PAM	pulse amplitude modulation
PBX	private branch exchange
PC	personal computer
PC	printed circuit
PCB	printed circuit board
PCI	Peripheral Component Interconnect
PCM	pulse code modulation

Table 7-1   *Abbreviations, Acronyms, and Units of Measurement* *(Continued)*

Abbreviation	Name or Term
PCMCIA	Personal Computer Memory Card International Association
PDL	page description language
PDL	program design language
PDM	pulse duration modulation
PDS	partitioned data set
PF	power factor
PHIGS	Programmer's Hierarchical Interactive Graphics System
PID	process identifier
PIO	programmed input/output
pixel	picture element
PLA	programmable logic array
p.m.	post meridiem (afternoon)
PMI	Protected Mode Interface
PMOS	positive-channel metal-oxide semiconductor
POSIX	Portable Operating System Interface for Computer Environments
POST	power-on self-test
ppb	parts per billion
ppm	parts per million
ppm	pages per minute
PPM	pulse position modulation
PPP	point-to-point protocol
PROM	programmable read-only memory
PS	power source
PU	power unit
R	
rad	radian
RAID	redundant array of inexpensive disks
RAM	random access memory
RC	resistance-capacitance
RCVR	receiver
RF	radio frequency

Table 7-1   *Abbreviations, Acronyms, and Units of Measurement (Continued)*

Abbreviation	Name or Term
RFI	radio frequency interference
RGB	red, green, blue
RISC	reduced instruction-set computer
RLL	run-length-limited
RO	receive only
ROM	read-only memory
RPC	remote procedure call
RTF	rich text format
RTL	resistor-transistor logic
R/W	read/write
RZ	return to zero
S	
s	second
sec	second
SAM	sequential access method
SAP	service access point
SCCS	Source Code Control System
SCN	specification change notice
SCR	silicon-controlled rectifier
SCSI	small computer system interface
SGML	Standard Generalized Markup Language
SHF	super-high frequency
SIMM	single in-line memory module
SIP	single in-line package
SLIP	serial-line Internet protocol
SLSI	super-large-scale integration
SMF	system management facilities
S/N	signal-to-noise ratio
SQL	structured query language
SRAM	static random access memory
SSI	small-scale integration

Table 7-1   *Abbreviations, Acronyms, and Units of Measurement (Continued)*

Abbreviation	Name or Term
SVGA	Super VGA
SWR	standing wave ratio
sync	synchronous
T	
T	tera (prefix)
TC	temperature coefficient
TCP	Transmission Control Protocol
TCP/IP	Transmission Control Protocol/Internet Protocol
TELEX	teletypewriter exchange
TIFF	tag image file format
TSO	timesharing option
TSR	terminate-and-stay-resident
TTL	transistor-transistor logic
TTY	teletypewriter
TWX	teletypewriter exchange service
U	
UART	universal asynchronous receiver-transmitter
UHF	ultra-high frequency
UID	user identification
ULSI	ultra-large-scale integration
UPS	uninterruptible power supply
URL	Uniform Resource Locator
U.S.	United States
USRT	universal synchronous receiver-transmitter
UUCP	UNIX-to-UNIX Copy
UV	ultraviolet
V	
V	volt
VAC	volts alternating current
VAR	value-added reseller
VCO	voltage-controlled oscillator

Table 7-1   Abbreviations, Acronyms, and Units of Measurement (Continued)

Abbreviation	Name or Term
VDC	volts direct current
VDT	video display terminal
VESA	Video Electronics Standards Association
VEU	volume end user
VF	voice frequency
VGA	video graphics adapter
VHF	very high frequency
VL	VESA local bus
VLB	VESA local bus
VLF	very low frequency
VLSI	very large scale integration
VRAM	video random access memory
VSAM	virtual sequential access method
W	
W	watt
WAIS	Wide-Area Information Server
WAN	wide-area network
Wh	watt-hour
WORM	write once, read many
WWW	World Wide Web

7

Read Me First!

Constructing Text 8≣

This chapter provides information about the use of text and graphics elements in your documents, such as section heads, tables, and cross-references. There are different ways to present these elements. The design, layout, and writing style that you choose will help to make your document unique.

The style and writing conventions in this chapter include suggestions that have worked successfully in published computer documents. You may decide to adopt these conventions, or to adapt them to your company's documentation. Whatever convention you choose, make sure that the format is easily recognized and understood by readers, and that you use your style consistently throughout a document.

This chapter discusses how to write and construct:

- Section heads
- Lists
- Steps and procedures
- Tables
- Code examples
- Error messages
- Cross-references
- Endnotes, footnotes, and bibliographies
- Notes, Cautions, and Warnings
- Part dividers
- Graphical user interfaces (GUIs)
- Typographic conventions

Section Heads

Heads concisely describe the material in the section that follows. No matter what their level, heads are not titles. *Heads* summarize information; *titles* name information.

The appropriate placement of document heads is dependent upon the content and flow of information, and sometimes on the page layout. For example, several pages of material may fit well within the context of a single level-one head, while a sentence or two may require a level-four head.

Writing Heads

Section heads should group topics within a chapter and provide a point of reference for a reader. Heads are hierarchical; you must carefully build heads and text in a logical and understandable progression. Level-one heads provide the broadest division, followed by level-two heads, and so on.

When writing heads:

* Make sure that the heads summarize the information discussed within a section.

  For example, in a section introducing a new type of modem to an end user, write "Speedway II Modem Features" rather than "Introduction."

* Use level-one heads for the broadest summaries, and become more specific as you progress to level-four heads. Don't go beyond level-four heads. Restructure the text, if necessary.

* Try to balance the placement of heads within a chapter.

  You may need to reorganize your text if there are three or more level-one heads on a single page. Also, try to have at least two heads at each level you're using.

* Try to use parallel grammar when writing heads at the same level.

  If a head level includes gerunds (for example, "Opening," "Installing"), then try to write all other heads at the same level with gerunds.

* Repeat the subject in the first sentence of the paragraph following a head, rather than using a pronoun to represent it.

      <Head2>Remote Digital Loopback

      Awkward: This tests the system's ability to . . . .

      Better: The remote digital loopback test examines . . . .

- Avoid starting heads with articles or with a technical term that begins with a lowercase letter. One exception is when programming commands are the only text used in the head.

- Don't repeat the exact text of higher-level heads in subheads.

Capitalizing and Punctuating Heads

The design of your document should include how you capitalize and punctuate section heads. The design you choose for heads should complement the design of chapter titles, and figure and table captions in your document. Some documents follow traditional rules of title capitalization for section heads, while others develop a unique look.

Following traditional guidelines for heads, you would:

- Use no punctuation at the ends of heads, except for a question mark when needed.

- Capitalize the first letter of all primary words in heads.

- Capitalize prepositions of four or more characters, or shorter ones if they appear at the beginning of the line or are an inseparable part of the verb (such as "Back Up" or "Spell Out").

- Use lowercase for the "to" in infinitives.

- Use lowercase for articles and conjunctions.

Following options for a unique design, you can:

- Use ordinary sentence punctuation if the heads are complete sentences.

- Capitalize only the first letter of the first word in heads.

- Use different type styles to establish the head hierarchy.

  For instance, you could:

  USE CAPS AND SMALL CAPS

  USE ALL CAPS

  Use an italic font

  ```
  Use an Alternative Font
  ```

Numbering Heads

Unnumbered heads are generally used within documents that are geared for end users, while *numbered heads* are reserved for more technical reference and service manuals.

Numbered section heads use the chapter number as the first digit. This digit is separated from the next digit, which represents the level-one head. The third digit represents the level-two head, followed by the digit for the level-three head, and so forth. All digits are separated by a delimiter, such as a period or an endash.

The section number 4.2.3.1 tells readers that the text is in Chapter 4, the second level-one head, the third level-two head, and the first level-three head. Sections would be numbered in this way:

4.2

    4.2.1

    4.2.2

    4.2.3

        4.2.3.1

Lists

Lists enable you to break out information from the paragraph format and put it into an easier-to-read format. Lists must comprise at least two entries. Be sure that your lists are unmistakably lists; that is, that they cannot be confused with steps, which denote actions. Although you may need to use secondary entries, remember that complex entries defeat the easy-to-read format of a list.

You can use unnumbered lists when the entries are not dependent upon the sequence in which you present them. These lists are often preceded by a symbol, such as a bullet (a solid circle) or a hollow or solid square.

When the entries are dependent upon sequence, use numerals and letters to build the hierarchy.

The design of your document should also specify how lists are aligned and spaced in relation to the paragraph text. You can place the symbol or numeral flush left under the preceding paragraph or indent it. For numbered lists, you also have formatting options, such as using an alternative font for the numbers and letters.

Introducing Lists

Introduce a list with one of the following:

- Sentence fragment that ends with a colon
- Sentence fragment that ends with no punctuation
- Complete sentence that ends with a colon
- Complete sentence that ends with a period
- Full paragraph

When you use a sentence fragment and a colon to introduce an unnumbered list, be sure that the syntax of the items in the list agrees with the syntax of the introduction, as shown in the next example.

Wrong:

You can send a mail message by:

- Compose a new one
- Reply to one sent to you
- Forward one

Right:

You can send a mail message by:

- Composing a new one
- Replying to one sent to you
- Forwarding one

When you use a complete sentence to introduce the list, decide whether the list entries flow naturally from the sentence. If so, use a colon. If the introductory sentence completes its information, use a period.

For example, you could use either of these statements to introduce the same list:

Send a mail message in any of the following three ways:

The operating system provides three convenient ways to send mail messages.

Capitalizing and Punctuating Lists

Be consistent when you construct the items in lists. Avoid mixing complete sentences and sentence fragments in the same list. In lists that mingle complete sentences with sentence fragments, a logical system of capitalization and punctuation becomes difficult to establish.

A simple style, which works well in computer documents, specifies that you:

- Capitalize the first word of each entry in the list.
- End sentence fragments with no punctuation.
- End all complete sentences with appropriate punctuation.

Writing Unnumbered Lists

Use unnumbered lists whenever the sequence of the entries is not important.

- Make sure that the items in unnumbered lists are similar in value.

  Wrong:

  The workstation you purchased comes with:

  - System unit
  - Monitor
  - Keyboard and mouse
  - Maybe a CD-ROM drive
  - Maybe a modem

  The last two entries in the example are not similar to the first three, because they are options, not standard equipment.

  Right:

  The workstation you purchased comes with a:

  - System unit
  - Monitor
  - Keyboard and mouse

  After setting up your workstation, you can add several options, such as a CD-ROM drive or modem.

- Use an introductory phrase for each entry, when needed.

  Lists sometimes begin with a summary word or phrase, followed by an explanation. In these cases, you have to define a format and type style for the lists. The next example shows a style that specifies the summary in italics, an en dash to separate the summary from the explanation, and a capital letter for the first word of the explanation.

  The workstation you purchased comes with:

  - *System unit* – This houses the . . . .
  - *Monitor* – This is a 19-inch . . . .
  - *Keyboard and mouse* – These are input . . . .

You could also present the summary in bold and end it with a period. The text that follows is in the same font as the document's body text. This style is often referred to as a *bold lead-in*; it works well when you have lengthy explanatory text for each entry.

The workstation you purchased comes with the following hardware:

System unit. This houses the . . . .

Monitor. This is a 19-inch . . . .

Keyboard and mouse. These are input . . . .

Writing Numbered Lists

Use numbered lists when the order of entries is important, but exercise caution. Many readers are impatient to complete tasks and could mistake numbered lists for procedures.

Write the text for numbered lists in a style that differs from steps and instructions. Don't assume that a reader will notice any format differences between numbered lists and numbered steps.

Avoid using verbs in the imperative form because they could lead a reader to believe that the numbered lists are a set of instructions. Use gerunds or participles instead. For example:

Wrong:

Creating a file with the vi editor involves four basic operations:

1. Start vi.

2. Add text to the file.

3. Write the file to save its contents.

4. Quit, or stop use of, vi.

To avoid possible misinterpretation, introduce the list clearly and don't use imperative verbs.

Right:

Creating a file with the vi editor involves four basic operations:

1. Starting vi

2. Adding text to the file

3. Writing the file to save its contents

4. Quitting vi

8

Steps and Procedures

Steps (instructions) comprise procedures and are sequential. Decide what a reader needs to do first, next, and last. Write clearly and number the steps so that a reader understands exactly what to do. Verbs do most of the work in instructions. Use imperatives when writing steps, and reserve participles and gerunds for lists.

Screen captures do not substitute for steps.

Introducing Steps

Introduce steps with one of the following constructions, making sure that you create an effective context for the procedure:

- Full paragraph
- Complete sentence that ends with a period
- Complete sentence that ends with a colon
- Sentence fragment that ends with a colon

Capitalizing and Punctuating Steps

Unlike lists, steps *always* should be complete sentences.

- Use sentence-style capitalization.
- End the sentence with appropriate punctuation.

Writing Steps

Use steps whenever you instruct a reader to complete a task.

- Never bury steps in a paragraph.
- Always use numerals and letters (for sub-steps) when a procedure comprises two or more steps.
- Use single-step procedures, when needed, but don't number them.

  If you assign a numeral "1" to a single-step procedure, a reader looks for "2" and may think you incorrectly omitted a second step. To avoid this, you can indicate a single-step procedure by replacing the "1" with a glyph, such as a solid triangle or an arrow before the step.

- If a reader must perform different actions depending upon the outcome of a step, use bullets to show the *alternatives* (use letters to show sub-steps).
- Determine the correct order in which to present the steps.
- Write each step as a complete, correctly punctuated sentence.

Read Me First!

- Begin steps with an active verb in the imperative form.

  For example, "Click the Open button." "Press the Standby switch to turn off the power."

- Provide as many visual cues to a reader as you can, and tell a reader what is supposed to happen after each step.

  For example, show a reader the screen that is displayed after successful completion of the step, or describe the screen.

- Don't combine two tasks into one step.

  An exception to this guideline is when you conclude a step with "and press Return," because that keystroke is a necessary component of the step. However, if all steps in a procedure conclude with "and press Return," you could inform a reader of this in the text that introduces the procedure, and eliminate the redundancy from the steps.

- Avoid redundancy in the text.

  For example, "check to make sure" is a redundancy that creeps into many steps. You don't need to tell the writer to "check," only to "make sure."

- Avoid cross-references in the instructions.

  When performing a task, readers may become frustrated if they have to frequently flip through pages or go to another document to find required information.

For example, a typical format for a procedure could be:

To open the disk drive enclosure:

1. **Remove the Phillips-head screw from the center rear of the drive.**

2. **Press in the tabs on the left and right sides of the enclosure.**

   The tabs are near the air vents on the enclosure.

3. **Remove the acoustic foam that covers the disk drive.**

   The foam has finger holes for you to use for quick removal.

8

Tables

Tables are an ideal format for presenting statistical information or facts that you can structure uniformly. Information that is conceptual or explanatory is best written in a narrative paragraph. Also, tables are easy for a reader to find when you list them in the table of contents.

Writing Text for Tables

Complex tables typically include a number, caption, column heads, and table text. Simple tables, such as those that list option flags and their descriptions, are often not numbered and have no captions. Use spaces and rules (vertical and horizontal lines) to format the table text.

Table Introductions

Introduce the context of a table to your readers.

- Refer to the table in the text that immediately precedes it.

  Refer to the table number ("Table 1-1 shows . . . .") rather than the table's position on the page ("The table below shows . . . .").

- Introduce the table with a complete sentence, not a phrase ending in a colon.

Table Captions

Writers usually choose a style for table captions that parallels the style used for section heads and figure captions.

When constructing table captions, consider how you will do the following:

- Number tables.

  Decide whether you want to use a single-digit (for example, "Table 1") or a double-digit (for example, Table 1-1) numbering system. The type of system you use should match the method you chose for the figure captions in your document.

- Indicate when table text runs onto more than one page.

  Many writers include the word "continued" in a caption that appears on the second and subsequent pages. Other writers may indicate a continued table by placing "continued" at the bottom of the table and a bottom rule only on the last page of the table text.

- Capitalize and punctuate table captions.

  Match the table caption style to the figure captions and section heads in your document.

Table Heads

Table heads concisely summarize information in a column.

- Avoid starting a table head with an article.

  For example, write "Alternative Backup Schedule" rather than "An Alternative Backup Schedule."

- Avoid end punctuation, except a question mark if required by the text.

- Capitalize and punctuate table heads as you do section heads.

Table Text

The table text is the main body of information, formatted into rows and columns.

- Use parallel construction, capitalization, and punctuation in the table text.

  For better readability, use an initial capital for only the first word in a cell, unless there is a reason to capitalize other words in the text.

- Avoid bold in table text, but use the typographic conventions established for the document.

- For footnotes in a table, use numerals whenever possible. When numerals might be confusing (due to numbers in the table text or many footnotes in text), use these symbols in the following order:
  - Asterisk (*)
  - Dagger (†)
  - Double-dagger (‡)
  - Section mark (§)

Determining the Type of Table to Use

Tables should present information in concise categories. There are several ways to design a table, depending upon the information you need to present. Table 8-1 is an example of a standard table with columns and rows separated by spaces.

Table 8-1   Standard Table

Specifier	Value of the Variable	Data Type for the Variable
ACCESS	'DIRECT SEQUENTIAL	CHARACTER
BLANK	'NULL' 'ZERO'	CHARACTER
IOSTAT	Error number	INTEGER
OPENED	.TRUE. .FALSE.	LOGICAL

Table 8-2 uses horizontal rules to group information into rows.

Table 8-2   Table With Horizontal Rules

Name and Address	Corporate Office	Sales	Service
ABC Corp. 624 Main Street Chelmsford, MA 01824	(617) 555-9731	(617) 555-1632	(617) 555-4932
DEF Corp. 90 Columbia Avenue Los Angeles, CA 94043	(213) 555-8413	(415) 555-5940	(415) 555-3662
GHI Corp. Colorado Springs, CO 80920	(719) 555-8842	(719) 555-9013	(719) 555-4701

Table 8-3 uses horizontal and vertical rules to separate information.

Table 8-3   Table With Horizontal and Vertical Rules

Command	Syntax	Options
at	at *time* at [*options*] *job-ids*	-l Lists current job. -r Removes specified job. *time* Time specified when commands will run.
chown	chown *owner filename*	-h Changes ownership of symbolic link.
find	find *filename*	-print Prints names of files found. -name *filename* Finds file with cited name.

Table 8-4 uses side and top heads to create a grid. Both the top and side heads are bold. A vertical rule separates the side heads from the table text.

Table 8-4   Table With Side and Top Heads

Permission	User	Group	Others
Read	4	4	4
Write	2	0	0
Execute	1	1	1
Total	7	5	5

Writing Text for Jump Tables

A *jump table* is a two-column table that serves as a table of contents for a portion of a book, usually for a chapter. If your document is on line, the jump table can include hypertext pointers to selected sections.

- Try to keep all the text of a jump table on the same page.
- Use jump tables consistently within your document.
- List heads that will be of particular interest to a reader.

Table 8-5 shows a jump table.

Table 8-5   Jump Table

To Set Up Automatic Data Collection	page 124
To Display Data Collection Statistics	page 152
To Display I/O Statistics	page 163
To Display Performance Statistics	page 179

Code Examples

Code examples are portions of computer programs that you include in your document to help explain a topic. Code examples can include only the code that a person inputs into the computer, or the dialogue between a user's input and the computer's responses.

Because programming code is precise, you must reproduce the exact code, even if there are language errors in the code, such as errors in spelling, grammar, or punctuation.

To make sure that a reader can distinguish the code from standard paragraph text, consider these writing and formatting techniques:

- Break out a code example from paragraph text.

  For instance, you can start an example on a new line, either flush under the paragraph text or indented. You can use a solid or dotted box around an example. You can use a color screen over your example, but be careful that it does not detract from readability.

- Use a caption for lengthy code examples.

  A caption highlights the example and categorizes it for a reader. If you use captions, you can compile a list of code examples in the table of contents.

- Use bold (or a different type style) to distinguish the user's input from the computer's response.

For example:

Code Example 8-1   Checking Status on the Tape Device

```
% mt -f /dev/rmt/0 status
Archive QIC-150 tape drive:
    sense key (0x0)= nosense  residual= 0   retries= 0
    file no= 0        block no= 0
```

Error Messages

Error messages are text strings that software provides to indicate that something is wrong with system software or hardware. When you explain error messages in your document, make sure that you copy the exact message.

- Format error messages in a way that differs from paragraph text.

- Always follow an error message with text describing why the message appears and what a reader can do to correct the problem.

- If you are documenting numerous error messages, consider compiling them into an appendix.

This is one way you can format error messages:

Error 50 - Internal Printer Malfunction

Caused By: Fusing assembly malfunction

Response: Turn off the printer for at least 15 minutes. If the error persists, a qualified technician must repair the printer.

Error 51 - Internal Printer Malfunction

Caused By: Beam detection malfunction

Response: Hold down the Alt key and click the Continue button to resume printing. If the error persists, a qualified technician must repair the printer.

Cross-References

Cross-references identify for a reader additional information about a specific topic that is available within the document or a different source. To be useful to a reader, cross-references must be specific and accurate. Include any detail that will help a reader find the information easily.

There are several acceptable formats for cross-references. These formats are often dependent upon where the cited information is located (within your document, another document produced by your company, or a third-party document) and the length of the reference.

However, you should never use a cross-reference:

- When the information is vital for a reader to understand the discussion

  Instead, provide the vital information. If the information is extensive, you can summarize it and also include a cross-reference to the source.

- When the additional information is brief and you can just as easily repeat it
- To cite the current page
- To cite safety information that describes how to protect a person, or hardware or software

  For safety information, use Caution or Warning text.

Fonts, Punctuation, and Capitalization

- Use an alternative font (usually italic) for the title of a book, journal, or magazine.

- Use quotation marks around a chapter or section head.

  Refer to Chapter 4, "System Board and Component Replacement," in *SPARCserver 1000 System Service Manual*.

- Capitalize "chapter," "appendix," "part," "section," "table," or "figure" when followed by a number or letter.

  Refer to Chapter 6, "Copying Files to a Diskette."

  . . . as shown in Figure 9, "Null Modem Cabling."

- Don't capitalize "page" or "step" when followed by a number.

  Go to step 4.

  Refer to page 42 for further information.

8

Writing Cross-References

Cross-references break the flow of your discussion, and therefore you should write them so that a reader easily recognizes when you have given a reference.

- Make sure that you introduce cross-references with clear phrases.

  Wrong: To reboot, see Chapter 4.

  Right: For instructions on how to reboot, see Chapter 4.

- If cross-references are brief, include them within the sentences. But if the cross-references require lengthy text references, put them in separate sentences.

  Use the `diff` *filename1 filename2* command to compare two files (see Section 1.2).

  Use the `diff` *filename1 filename2* command to compare two files. See Section 1.2, "Working With Text Files," in Chapter 2 of *UNIX Simplified*.

Cross-References to Third-Party Documents

- For a cross-reference to a third-party book, include the title and author, with the publisher and year in parentheses.

  One of the reference books used in preparation of this document was *The Deluxe Transitive Vampire* by Karen Elizabeth Gordon (Pantheon Books, 1993).

- Do not use a cross-reference to a specific chapter or section of a third-party book.

Cross-References to Text Within Your Document

You can provide a cross-reference to a part, chapter, appendix, section, figure, or table within your book.

- Don't provide the title of your document as part of the cross-reference.

  See Chapter 4, "Closing the System Unit Cover."

  Go to Section 3.3.2, "Reserving Disks," in Chapter 3, "Getting Started."

- If you repeat a cross-reference within the same chapter of your document, you don't have to repeat the title of the part, chapter, appendix, section, figure, or table after its first reference.

  For example, here are shortened versions of the previous example:

  See Chapter 4.

  . . . as described in Section 3.3.2.

Cross-References to Another Document Produced by Your Company

- For a cross-reference to another book produced by your company, include your company's name, the book's title, and part number.

     Refer to Intellicon's *Administrator's Guide for X Terminal Software*, part number 690-32-1146.

- If the book is part of the same product set, or is packaged with the product, the book title alone is sufficient.

Endnotes, Footnotes, and Bibliographies

Sometimes you may need to provide complete cross-references to other sources. You can include these references in *endnotes* at the end of a chapter, in *footnotes* at the bottom of a page, or in a *bibliography* at the end of the document. Writers also use endnotes and footnotes as a place to add comments about a discussion.

Writing Endnotes and Footnotes

Endnotes and footnotes provide complete information about the source, including author, title, place of publication, and the page number in the source where readers can find the information. A footnote provides the reference at the bottom of the page, while an endnote groups all references cited within a chapter at the end of the chapter.

- Use consecutive superscript numerals in the main text to indicate the endnotes or footnotes.

     Place the numeral at the end of the sentence, phrase, or quotation for which you are providing a reference. Don't include a period after the superscript numeral. The numeral appears after punctuation marks, except for a dash.

- Avoid using lettered sub-notes, such as 4a and 4b.

- Keep the text of the footnote on the same page as its superscript numeral.

- Don't place endnote or footnote numerals in chapter or section titles, or in figure or table captions.

- Introduce the text of the note with the corresponding numeral, followed by a period. Use consistent alignment of the numerals and text. Single space the text of each note, and add extra space between notes.

- When repeatedly referring to the same source document, you can abbreviate the information. Include only the author's last name, the book title, and the page number.

Here are some examples of the content and style of endnotes and footnotes:

1. Skillin, Marjorie E., Robert M. Gay, and other authorities. *Words into Type*, 3d ed. Englewood Cliffs, New Jersey: Prentice-Hall, 1974, p. 150.

2. Burnett, Rebecca E., *Technical Communication*, 2d ed. Belmont, California: Wadsworth Publishing Company, 1990, p. 36.

3. *The Chicago Manual of Style*, 14th ed. Chicago: University of Chicago Press, 1993, p. 701.

4. Skillin, *Words into Type*, p. 16.

Writing Bibliographies

A bibliography lists all sources that you refer to in your document. It appears at the end of the document, following the appendixes and before the index.

The format for bibliographies varies depending upon the number and type of resources cited (books, journals, articles, and so forth). *The Chicago Manual of Style* provides a lengthy discussion on text and formats used in bibliographies. Its guidelines are summarized below.

When citing a book, provide the following information:

- Name of the person or institution credited as author (this may be a single or multiple authors, editors, or institutions)
- Full title of the source, including any subtitle
- Title of the series, and its volume and number if the book is part of a series
- Volume number, if the book is part of a multivolume set
- Edition of the book, if it is not the original edition
- City where the book was published
- Publisher's name
- Date of publication

For an article in a periodical, provide the following information:

- Name of the author
- Title of the article
- Name of the periodical
- Volume or issue number of the periodical
- Date of the periodical
- Page numbers where the article is found in the periodical

Here are two examples of ways to format text for bibliographies. The first example wraps each line flush left, while the second example provides a two-column format.

> Atre, Anand. *Performance Tuning Guide for Sybase SQLserver on Solaris.* Mountain View, CA: Sun Microsystems, Inc., 1995.

> Yram, Kaytram.   *Upgrading Your System With Multimedia.* Acton, MA: New Look Publishing, 1995.

When citing electronic source material, provide the following information:

- Name of the author, plus the author's email address if available
- Title of the work or the title line of the message
- Title of the list/site as appropriate
- Volume or issue number of a digest, if applicable
- Date of the message or the date the source was accessed
- Page or screen numbers where the article is found, if applicable

Here are some examples of suggested ways to format the various types of electronic sources.

- Database on line

  Joe User, "Citing Electronic Material," in REFSTUFF [database on line] (Silicon, Calif.: REFSTUFF, 1986) [updated 9 January 1996; cited 31 February 1996], identifier no. Q000307. [52 lines.]

- Email messages

  Joe User [juser@macland.org], "Citing Electronic Material," private email message to Sis Admin [sadmin@funix.com], 31 February 1996.

- FTP site

  Joe User [juser@macland.org], "Citing Electronic Material," [ftp.macland.org/pub/local/reference/cites.txt], February 1996.

- Listserv message

  Joe User [juser@macland.org], "REPLY: Citing Electronic Material," in GRAMR, (Digest vol. 6, no. 8) [electronic bulletin board] (Dubuque, Iowa, 1995 [cited 31 February 1996)]; available from gramr@miskatonic.edu]; INTERNET.

- World Wide Web

  Joe User, "Citing Electronic Material," [http://www.macland.org/cites.html], accessed 31 February 1996.

Notes, Cautions, and Warnings

Notes, Cautions, and Warnings provide important information that diverges from the topic under discussion. A Note, Caution, or Warning is preceded with a strong visual cue, which draws a reader's attention to the text.

A *Note* usually provides related, parenthetical information, such as an explanation, tip, comment, or other useful, but not imperative, information. However, overuse of Notes is a sign of unorganized writing. If a page contains three or more Notes, decide whether you can incorporate some of the Note text into the paragraph text.

Cautions and *Warnings* are mandatory text that you *must* provide to protect the user of equipment from personal injury, or to protect hardware or software from damage. In most computer documents, writers precede the text of Cautions and Warnings with graphical symbols that are specified by the International Organization for Standardization (ISO). These internationally accepted symbols were designed to alert the person working with software or handling equipment about important information.

Writing Notes

There are few constraints on the text or format you can use in a Note. Consistency in both writing style and format is important so that a reader learns to recognize a Note interjected into the text.

Some guidelines:

- Use a Note to break out related, reinforcing, interesting, or other "special" information that you want to be sure a reader sees.
- Keep your Note short and relevant.
- Never use a Note to cite safety information.

Here are examples of Note formats.

Note – This is an example of a Note. There are many ways in which you can format the text. However, keep the text short and relevant.

This is another example of a Note. Hints and tips work well in this format. Be brief.

Read Me First!

Writing Cautions

Unlike a Note, a Caution is not optional.

- You *must* use a Caution whenever anything you describe poses possible damage to equipment, data, or software.

- Be direct when writing a Caution. Describe the potential hazard, the data or machinery that may be damaged, and the measures that a reader can take to guard against the damage.

- Add a visual cue, such as the internationally accepted exclamation point inside a triangle, to make sure that a reader sees the Caution.

Here are examples of Cautions.

 Caution – Lithium batteries are not customer-replaceable parts. Do not disassemble them or attempt to recharge them.

Caution – Software hazard is present. Before copying data from a disk from an outside source, check the disk for viruses. Otherwise, you may contaminate the data on your hard disk.

Writing Warnings

Warnings, like Cautions, are not optional.

- You *must* use a Warning whenever you describe a situation that poses personal injury to a person, or when there is a risk of irreversible destruction to data or the operating system.

- Make sure that your documentation meets all government regulatory standards for the mandated use of Warnings.

- Write directly to the point, in plain and clear language. Explain what could go wrong if a reader does not follow the instructions precisely.

- Explain the risk and advise a reader how to avoid the risk.

- Use the "lightning bolt" symbol when there is danger of physical harm to a person or damage to equipment due to an electrical hazard.

- Use the "heat" symbol when there is risk of personal injury from a heat source.

- Use the "exclamation point" symbol when there is risk of personal injury from a nonelectrical hazard, or risk of irreversible damage to data, software, or the operating system.

Here are some examples of Warnings.

 Warning – Electrical hazard is present. Leaving the side panel off the computer exposes you to dangerous voltage and risk of electrical shock. Do not leave the side panel off while you are operating the computer.

 Warning – Hot surface. The surface of the CPU chip may be hot and could cause personal injury if touched. Do not touch this component.

 Warning – Risk of personal injury is present. Do not move this cabinet without help. The server weighs more than 500 kilograms. The assistance of at least three people is needed to move the server.

 Warning – There is risk of irreversible destruction to data or the operating system. Follow the instructions carefully.

Part Dividers

Lengthy books may require *part dividers* to group similar chapters within the document. Because readers often merely glance at the part divider page, keep the text on the divider page minimal and succinct.

Never include any information on the divider that is essential to the topic discussed in the chapters. For example, instructions to turn off the power before proceeding with the tasks in the chapters are not appropriate on the divider. However, an explanation of why the chapters are grouped into a part could be helpful to a reader.

Typically, when you prepare part dividers for computer documentation:

- Make sure that you have at least two parts.
- Provide a part number and title.

  Organizations vary in their choice of using either Arabic or Roman numerals for the part number.

- Include only text, or text with graphics.

  For example, you could use graphics on the front of the part divider with text on the back, or a combination of text and graphics on the front with text continuing on the back.

- List the chapter titles on the divider to orient a reader; for on-line documents, include a hypertext jump table of the chapter titles.

- Do not include a page number on the part divider page

  Although a page number does not appear on the part divider, the divider is counted in the total number of pages of the document.

Graphical User Interfaces

A *graphical user interface* (GUI) provides the user with an intuitive way of interacting with a computer and its applications. The main purpose of a GUI is to make the activities involved in doing a task simple and quick. Common GUIs require a person to use a mouse or some other pointing and selecting device. GUIs are typically built around *windows*, which provide a simple means to manipulate files and directories. *Icons*, which are small pictorial representations of a base window, are often used to simplify access to a program, command, or data file.

Using GUI Terminology

Although many computer users today are very familiar with GUIs, you may still need to explain to novice computer users the basic concepts of the GUI and how to work in it. In the preface, define terms you use throughout your document, such as "point," "click," "double-click," "select," or "choose." You also can provide a figure of a typical window to clarify terms.

Once you have established how to work in a GUI, you can concentrate on writing about the task the user wants to accomplish, not on describing the detailed steps required to initiate the task. For example, a user rarely chooses menu items or clicks buttons with the goal of displaying other menus or dialog boxes, but rather to accomplish a task that is activated by the menu item or button.

When writing about GUIs:

- Provide only the essential details or information that the user needs to know to accomplish the task.

- Distinguish windows, dialog boxes, and menus by using their proper names, but avoid repeated use of the same name when the meaning is clear.

  For example, if you've told the user to choose Print from the File menu and the Print window is displayed, and you want them to work in the Print window, there's no need to keep saying "in the Print window."

- Mention certain technical GUI distinctions only when necessary.

  For example, mention that a menu is a *pop-up menu* or a message is a *status message* only if that information is germane to the task at hand.

When writing about a mouse, note that:

- The buttons on the mouse are referred to as *mouse buttons* to avoid confusion with control or command buttons in application windows.

- The indicator that shows where the mouse action occurs is called the *pointer* or *cursor*.

  Keep the user's attention focused on the screen by writing about the pointer, not the mouse, even though a user moves the pointer on the screen by moving the mouse.

- The plural for "mouse" is "mouse devices."

Writing About Windows, Menus, and Dialog Boxes

A GUI includes the basic elements in which the application displays text and the user interacts with the application: windows, window controls, dialog boxes, and menus. Figure 8-1 and Figure 8-2 show common window elements and controls.

Window Elements

A *window* is the main, rectangular area in which application elements are displayed. The elements in a window vary from application to application.

- *Background* – Bordered rectangle in which the application displays its data or the user enters data

- *Control area* – Region of a window where controls, such as buttons or settings, are displayed

- *Footer* – Region in which the application displays status and error messages, or state and mode information

- *Header* – Region in which the application displays a title as a long-term message

- *Icon* – Pictorial representation of a base window

- *Pop-up window* – Window that provides related information

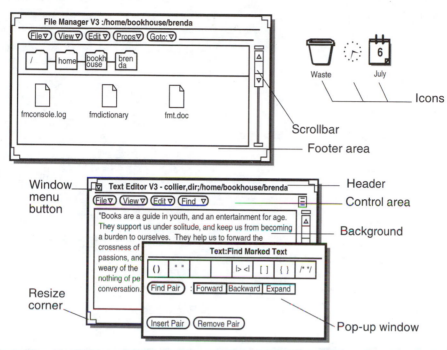

Figure 8-1   *Window Elements*

Window Controls

Controls in windows enable the user to perform an action. These are some common window controls:

- *Button* – Small area within the base window on which the user clicks to execute commands (command button), display pop-up windows (window button), or display menus (menu button)

- *Scrollbar* – Control that moves the view of the data displayed in the window

- *Resize corner* – Control that enables the user to resize the window without changing the scale of the contents

- *Check box* – A yes/no or on/off control; a check mark usually appears in the square check box when a setting is selected

- *Radio button* – A yes/no or on/off control; usually, only one radio button in a group can be selected

- *Gauge* – A read-only control that shows the percentage of use or the portion of an action that has been completed

- *Slider* – Control that is used to set a value and give a visual indication of the setting

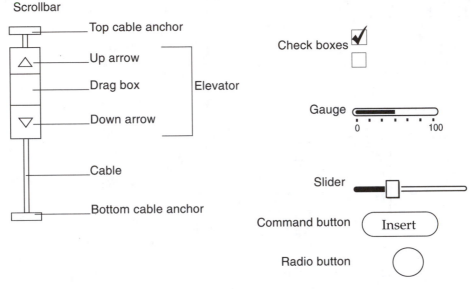

Scrollbar

Top cable anchor

Up arrow

Drag box

Elevator

Down arrow

Cable

Bottom cable anchor

Check boxes

Gauge

0   100

Slider

Command button   Insert

Radio button

Figure 8-2   Window Controls

Dialog Boxes

A *dialog box* is a pop-up window in which the user enters information or commands to the application. Figure 8-3 shows various types of dialog boxes.

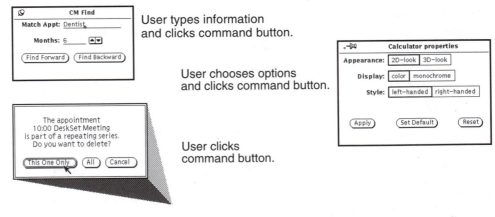

CM Find

Match Appt: Dentist

Months: 6

Find Forward   Find Backward

User types information and clicks command button.

User chooses options and clicks command button.

Calculator properties

Appearance: 2D–look   3D–look

Display: color   monochrome

Style: left–handed   right–handed

Apply   Set Default   Reset

The appointment 10:00 DeskSet Meeting is part of a repeating series. Do you want to delete?

This One Only   All   Cancel

User clicks command button.

Figure 8-3   Dialog Boxes

Menus

A *menu* or a *submenu* is a list of application options, as shown in Figure 8-4.

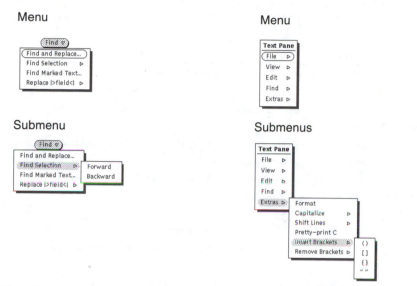

Figure 8-4   Menus and Submenus

When you first write about choosing items or settings from a menu, use step-by-step instructions. If an option name includes an ellipsis mark, do not include the ellipsis mark when mentioning the menu item in text.

Here is an example of steps that use menu options.

> To paste text:

1. Press the left mouse button on the Edit button in the menu bar.

> The Edit menu is displayed.

2. Drag the pointer to the Paste item and release the mouse button.

> The contents of the clipboard are placed at the insertion point.

After you have explained how menus work, you can streamline the process by saying "Choose Paste from the Edit menu."

Common GUI Verbs

When writing about GUIs, reserve certain verbs for specific activities, as described in Table 8-6.

Table 8-6   GUI Verbs

Verb	Action	Example
Choose	To open a menu or initiate a command.	Choose New from the File menu. Save your file, and then choose Print.
Click	To press and release a mouse button without moving the pointer.	Click the left mouse button.
Copy	To place a duplicate of the selection on the clipboard.	Copy the first figure in Appendix B.
Cut	To remove the selection from the current location and place it on the clipboard.	Cut the second entry in the list.
Dismiss	To close a window.	Dismiss the Shell Tool window.
Display	To open a window.	Display the Default Properties window.
Double-click	To click a mouse button twice quickly without moving the pointer.	Double-click on the Mosaic icon to reopen the program.
Drag	To move the pointer or an object by sliding the mouse with one or more buttons pressed.	Drag the pointer to draw a text box. Drag the icon to the upper-left corner of the screen.
Move	To move the pointer on the workspace by sliding the mouse with no buttons pressed.	Move the pointer outside of the Mail window.
Open	To start an application, or to access a document, file, or folder.	Open the FrameMaker icon. Open the Samples document.
Paste	To place the clipboard contents at the insertion point.	Paste the figure into Chapter 3.
Point	To move the pointer to a specific location on the screen by moving the mouse with no buttons pressed. (Once the user is familiar with mouse techniques, you do not have to use this term; you can simply write "Click the Trash icon.")	Point to the Trash icon and click to select it.

Table 8-6   *GUI Verbs (Continued)*

Verb	Action	Example
Press	To push a mouse button down and hold it. (Don't say "press and hold down" since the action of pressing includes holding down the button.)	Press the left mouse button on the File button.
Release	To let up on a mouse button to initiate an action.	Release the left mouse button when the Print button is highlighted.
Select	To highlight an entire window or data in a window.	Select the Compose window. Select the second sentence.
Size	To enlarge or decrease the size of a window.	Size the Text Editor window so that you can display more characters per line.

Typographic Conventions

Typographic conventions help a reader distinguish special uses of words. When you select typographic conventions for computer documentation, you have some decisions to make. These decisions are dependent upon the type of hardware or software that you are documenting.

Make sure that you consider these factors when selecting conventions:

- A set of conventions already may be specified and used as a standard within the computer industry for your type of document.

  For example, documents about hardware or software that is compatible with Macintosh systems often follow conventions defined by Apple Computer, Inc.

- If you design a unique set of conventions, make sure that the type is easily recognized and understood by readers, and that you explain how the conventions are used in the document.

8

Assigning Conventions to Text

There are no right or wrong typographic conventions, unless the type you choose is illegible or you mix too many fonts on a page. Most typography errors occur when writers do not apply conventions consistently. Here are some elements used in computer documentation for which you may want to establish type conventions:

- File names, directory names, path names, commands, and variables
- Generic classes of file names; for example, UNIX swap files or make files
- Menu names and menu commands in a graphical user interface
- Text you want the user to type
- Simultaneous keystrokes
- Consecutive keystrokes
- Menu names and menu commands in a TTY interface
- New terms, emphasized words, and foreign terms

Working With Conventions

To help readers understand the typographic conventions you use in a document, explain and demonstrate the type conventions in the preface.

For example, if you do not need to specify many conventions for your document, you could format the explanation in the preface this way.

This book uses the following type conventions:

- New terms and book titles appear in *italic* type.
- Text that you type, when shown alongside an example of computer output, is shown in **`bold Courier font`**.
- Text that appears on the screen, such as a computer response or a file name, is shown in `Courier font`.
- Names of keys on the keyboard appear with initial capitals, such as the Return key.
- Two key names joined with a hyphen are simultaneous keystrokes. Press down the first key while you type the second character, as in press Stop-a."
- Two key names joined with a plus sign are consecutive keystrokes. Press down the first key, release it, then type the second character, as in press F4+q.

Read Me First!

You could present a more formal explanation of text conventions in a table format, as done in Table 8-7.

Table 8-7   Typographic Conventions

Typeface or Symbol	Meaning	Example
AaBbCc123	The names of commands, files, and directories; on-screen computer output	Edit your `.login` file. Use `ls -a` to list all files. *machine_name%* `You have mail.`
AaBbCc123	What you type, contrasted with on-screen computer output	*machine_name%* **su** `Password:`
AaBbCc123	Command-line placeholder; replace with a real name or value	To delete a file, type `rm` *filename*.
AaBbCc123	Book titles, new words or terms, or emphasized words	Read Chapter 6 in *User's Guide*. These are called *class* options. You *must* be root to do this.
C shell prompt		*machine_name%*
C shell superuser prompt		*machine_name#*

Tables 8-8 and 8-9 present conventions, with examples, that you could use to identify text elements. Table 8-8 includes conventions that are used to construct a basic document; Table 8-8 includes conventions that are specific to computer documentation.

Table 8-8   Typographic Conventions for Basic Document Design

Text	Typeface or Symbol	Example
Book titles	Palatino italic	See *DeskSet Reference Guide*.
Head1	Palatino 15-point regular italic	*Head1 Example*
Head2	Palatino 14-point regular italic	*Head2 Example*
Head3	Palatino 13-point regular italic	*Head3 Example*
Head4	Palatino 11-point bold italic	***Head4 Example***
Paragraphs	Palatino 10-point regular	This is a paragraph.
Table captions	Palatino 9-point italic	*Table 1-1 Caption Text*
Table captions continued	Palatino 9-point italic	*Table 1-1 Caption Text (Continued)*
Table heads	Palatino 9-point bold	**Table Head**
Table text	Palatino 9-point regular	Table Text
Figure captions	Palatino 9-point italic	*Figure 1-1 Caption Text*
Figure callouts	Helvetica 9-point regular	This is a callout.
Chapter or section names	Palatino in quotation marks	See Chapter 1, "Getting Started."
Emphasized or new words	Palatino italic	You *must* be the root user to do this. These are called *class* options.
Foreign terms	Palatino italic	The user's *laissez-faire* attitude.
Glossary terms	Palatino bold for term, regular for definition, and italic for cross-reference	**read-only memory (ROM)** System memory that contains permanent instructions. See also *memory*.

Table 8-9   *Typographic Conventions for Technical Design*

Text	Typeface or Symbol	Example
Command names or options; directory, file, or path names; and code examples	Courier	Edit your `.login` file. Type `ls -a` to list all files.
User input contrasted with computer output, or prompt in code boxes	Courier bold to distinguish from computer output	*system%* **su** `Password:`
Variable, command-line placeholder	Palatino italic	Type `cd` *directory_name*
Options, command-line placeholders	[Palatino italic] Enclosed by brackets and separated by a vertical bar	Order by [*ASC*|*DESC*]
Key names and key cap abbreviations	Palatino initial cap for full names	Press Escape. Press the Control key.
	All caps for abbreviations	Press ESC. Press CTRL.
Simultaneous keystrokes	Joined with a hyphen	Shift-F1 means to hold down the Shift key while pressing the F1 key.
Consecutive keystrokes	Joined with a plus sign	ALT+ F+A means to press and release each key in the given order.
Man pages referred to in running text	Courier	See the `write(1)` man page.
Menu items, menu names	Palatino	Choose Go To from the Page menu.
Settings in windows	Palatino	Check the Pair Kern setting.
Window button names	Palatino	Click Apply to save changes.
Arrow keys	Palatino	.Up arrow, left arrow

The point size of the font for these elements should match the point size of the text within which they appear; for example, within a head, paragraph, table, or caption.

8

Read Me First!

Indexing 9 ≡

An index is often the readers' primary information retrieval device. When readers search for a particular topic and find it referenced in an index, they are assured that the topic is covered in the document and need look no further. When, on the other hand, readers don't find it in an index, they may decide that the topic is not covered in that document and look elsewhere.

In surveys of readers of technical documents, many complain about the inability to find the information they are seeking. An index goes a long way toward solving the problem of locating information.

This chapter describes how to prepare an index for a technical manual. The following topics are of particular importance in this chapter:

- An introduction to indexing
- Style and format
- Creating an index
- Editing an index
- The global index

Note – This chapter makes recommendations, but there are many other acceptable styles and theories of indexing.

What Is an Index?

According to *The Chicago Manual of Style*:

> A good index records every pertinent statement made within the body of the text. The key word here is *pertinent*. The subject matter and purpose of the book determine which statements are pertinent and which statements are peripheral. An index should be considerably more than an expanded table of contents and considerably less than a concordance of words and phrases.[1]

Style and Format

Figure 9-1 shows two examples of the *indented* indexing style (as opposed to the *run-in* style). One example shows the index format for unnumbered chapters, the other example is for numbered chapters. The only differences between the two examples are the format of the page numbers and the use of "to" as a separator for page ranges in the book with numbered chapters.

Unnumbered chapter format example:

A

application architecture, 12
application gateway, **211**, 345–351
automounter facility, 49–54
    See also mounting
    overview, 49
    setup, 51
        remote mounting, 52
        specifying subdirectories, 51

B

backing up
    file systems, 58
        dump command, 89–92
        dump strategies, 81
    servers, 83

Numbered chapter format example:

A

application architecture, 1-2
application gateway, **4-18**, 5-76 to 5-81
automounter facility, 2-12 to 2-18
    See also mounting
    overview, 2-12
    setup, 2-15
        remote mounting, 2-16
        specifying subdirectories, 2-14

B

backing up
    file systems, 3-1
        dump command, 3-34 to 3-37
        dump strategies, 3-26
    servers, 3-28

Figure 9-1   Index Formats

---

1. *The Chicago Manual of Style*, 14th ed. (Chicago: University of Chicago Press, 1993), p. 703.

Nested Entries

Many technical documents use up to three levels of nested entries: *primary* entry, *secondary* entry, and *tertiary* entry. Each entry level is indented from the previous level. These three levels appear as follows:

> primary entry
>> secondary entry
>>> tertiary entry

The primary entry is the principal subdivision of an index. A simple primary entry comprises the entry and a page number. A primary entry comprising several page numbers is usually divided into secondary entries. Each secondary entry must bear a logical relationship to the primary entry. A secondary entry comprising several page numbers may be further divided into tertiary entries. Each tertiary entry must bear a logical relationship to the secondary entry.

In indented style, each secondary entry and each tertiary entry begins a new indented line (unless there is only one secondary entry). If an entry runs over the width of the column, it is indented. This is known as a *flush-and-hang* style. For entries longer than the column width, the first line is set flush and the rest of the entry is indented below it.

> Least-Recently-Used (LRU) Ring functional
>> description, 3-17
>> elements of, 3-24

Page Number Style

A common indexing style calls for a comma and a space to be inserted between the entry and the first page number. Subsequent page numbers are separated with a comma and a space. Page numbers appear in ascending order.

Often, the primary entry that has two or more secondary entries does not have any page reference itself.

> functional description
>> input block, 2-3
>> introduction, 2-1
>> output block, 2-33

Major Page References

In certain cases, you may want to identify a particular page as the main source of information for a given topic, especially if the topic cites two or more pages. You can identify the main page by marking the page number in bold.

> dragging operations, 13, **37**, 114

Page Ranges

In an inclusive page reference spanning several pages, there are two common styles: first and last page numbers separated with an en dash (–); or a space, the word "to," and another space if you include the chapter number as part of the page number.

> screen adjustments, 6–12
> screen adjustments, 1-6 to 1-12

"See" and "See Also" References

Here are basic formatting rules for "See" and "See also" references. (There are also other acceptable styles.)

Italicize the words "See" and "See also."

> base window, 45
> > *See also* pane

Place the "See" reference on the same line as the index entry.

> search, *See* find

"See" and "See also" references should never include page numbers. Use these references to direct a reader to another entry.

> floppy, *See* diskette

"See also" references should appear at the beginning of the entry. Place the "See also" reference on a line by itself, and indent the reference from the line above.

> aggregation scheme
> > *See also* summarization, data

For more information, read the section "Creating "See" and "See Also" References" on page 162.

Capitalization

Do not capitalize any word in an index entry, unless the word is a proper noun, an acronym, or an abbreviation that is supposed to be capitalized. Use standard rules for capitalization.

> subwindow command, 37
> View accelerator, 34

Punctuation

If an entry is followed immediately by page references, insert a comma between the entry and the first page reference, and between subsequent page references.

> scrolling, 12, 16, 27

Punctuate an inverted phrase to show the inversion.

> function keys, right-handed, 21
> text facility, editing functions, 7

No punctuation is used between a primary entry without page numbers and subsequent secondary entries.

> selection
> > adjusting, 64
> > extending, 59

Use a semicolon to separate multiple "See also" and "See" references.

> local-area network
> > *See also* Ethernet; standards, networking

Special Typography

The index is subject to many of the same typographic style conventions found in the text of the document itself. For example, if file names and commands appear in Courier typeface in your book, then they should appear that way in the index.

> `dump` command, 28
> `core` file, 16
> `rlogin` problem, 166

Other types of special typography you might use in an index include bold for main page references and italics for "See" and "See also" references.

Creating an Index

Indexing is an iterative process. Your first pass at an index is merely the foundation on which to build your final index. The first pass will be full of similar primary entries that you need to break into secondary entries. You will probably also have problems with page ranges and spelling. See "Editing an Index" on page 170 for information about possible problems.

When an Index Is Needed

A document needs an index if it has 10 or more pages. This rule applies to any type of document, from simple end-user guides to technical reference manuals.

9

Time Required to Create an Index

Writers usually set aside less time for preparing an index than for almost any other step in the process of creating a document. Most writers can't (or shouldn't) work on an index until the document is written. At that point, people are anxious to get their hands on the document and time is rapidly running out.

As a rule of thumb, allow one full day for every 25 pages of text. A 100-page document will take four full days to index. An experienced indexer may require less time; a first-time indexer may require more time. Certain types of documents are much more difficult to index than others and require even more time than given in this guideline.

Note – If you have your book's index prepared by a professional indexer using dedicated indexing software, approximately 50 to 60 pages of technical material can be indexed per day.

Deciding Which Parts of a Document to Index

The first decision you need to make when starting to create an index is to determine which parts of a document to index.

- *Front matter* – The title page, copyright page, table of contents, and lists of figures and tables should not be indexed.

- *Preface* – You should index the preface if it contains information about the subjects within the document, and not just why the document was written. Topics you might index in a preface include prerequisite knowledge, other applicable documents, a description of the intended audience, or document conventions.

- *Chapters* – Use the main body of the document as the source for most of the index entries.

- *Tables and figures* – Topics within tables and figures should be indexed when they are of particular importance to the discussion. Items within tables that merely reproduce information already contained in the text should not be indexed. Index references to the tables and figures themselves often are very helpful to a reader.

- *Footnotes* – Footnotes may be indexed if they contain information that expands on the information in the text. Footnotes that merely document statements in the text should not be indexed.

- *Appendixes* – Appendixes should be indexed if they contain pertinent material omitted from the main body of the document, but not if they merely reproduce information already contained in the main body. A quick reference in an appendix, for example, is usually not indexed. Nor is a questionnaire. Worksheets in an appendix, unless they are merely repeated from the main text, are indexed.

- *Back matter* – Normally, terms in a glossary should not be indexed, as long as they are explained elsewhere in the document. A bibliography and a reader comment form should not be indexed.

Selecting Topics to Index

When you take on the task of creating an index, you must first decide what the pertinent statements or topics are. A topic can be a single word, a phrase, or even a concept. A topic has no minimum or maximum size.

As you analyze a topic for inclusion in your index, decide whether the topic contains information a reader may expect to find in the index. If it does, create one or more index entries.

To determine whether a topic requires an index entry, analyze the topic for the following attributes. Create an index entry when a topic:

- *Describes how to perform a task* – Tasks are the key subjects in certain types of documents, such as installation manuals.

- *Contains a definition of a term* – Definitions are frequently the key to a reader's understanding of the information in a document. Therefore, an index should make it easy for a reader to find the definition.

- *Is an acronym or abbreviation* – The meanings of acronyms and abbreviations are similar to definitions.

- *States a restriction, such as a Caution or Warning* – Awareness of the restriction might help a reader avoid making a costly or annoying mistake.

- *Explains a concept or an idea* – This type of topic is most helpful to a reader; however, creating the index entries that describe a concept or an idea is fairly difficult. The difficulty is in trying to describe the whole concept in a few words.

Don't Index Superfluous Entries

Frequently, superfluous entries are included in an index because the person creating the index erroneously refers to every occurrence of selected words or phrases in the document. The index is not a concordance, but rather an information retrieval device.

For example, assume that the following sentence appeared in the text being indexed:

> Separate chapters of this manual are devoted to the use of disk and tape storage devices.

In this example, the sentence provides no information about disk or tape storage. Therefore, a reader would gain nothing from these index entries:

> disk storage, 37
>
> .
>
> .
>
> tape storage, 37

Those entries should be included in an index only if they refer a reader directly to useful information.

Avoid Overly Global Entries

Do not use entries that are so general that they will apply to a global level of information. Such an entry is too general to inform a reader of the entry's corresponding content in the text.

For example, don't include entries such as "File Manager, creating files in" in a book about File Manager; or "features, of Lotus 1-2-3" in a book about the Lotus 1-2-3® application. Generally the only entries under the name of the application you're documenting should deal with the actual application itself, such as installing or quitting it.

Include Common Industry Terminology

Common procedures or commands may be defined by different terms depending upon the technology or company. If you know of a common synonym for a process or command, include an entry to send a reader to the term used in your book, as shown in these examples:

> search, *See* find
>
> delete, *See* cut
>
> abort, *See* cancel

Avoid Using Headings as Index Entries

Many writers choose to index every section head in the document. In general, you shouldn't use headings as the sole basis for an index. When you want to include the basic information contained in a heading in an index entry, avoid such entries as:

> using direct virtual memory access (DVMA), 87
> running the QuickView utility, 42
> What is a hidden file?, 28

Instead use entries such as these:

> direct virtual memory access (DVMA), using, 87
> QuickView utility, running, 42
> hidden file, definition, 28

Describing a Topic

Once you have determined that a topic merits an index entry, find one or more ways to describe it to a reader. The descriptions you create become the subjects of the index entries.

To describe a topic:

- Anticipate a reader's needs.
- Select the proper words for the subjects.
- Arrange the words for emphasis.
- Create multiple entries (double-post).
- Group the entries.

While looking for and describing topics, don't forget to create entries for Notes, Cautions, Warnings, acronyms, and abbreviations.

Anticipate a Reader's Needs

When a reader goes to an index, it is usually to answer one of the following questions:

- Where can I find information about a certain task, term, or topic?
- Which pages can I ignore because they contain information I already know?
- Does the information described by an index entry tell me what something is, how it works, or how to use it?

By anticipating a reader's needs as you describe topics for your index, you can avoid many of the pitfalls of an inadequate index.

9

Include Only Terms a Reader Is Likely to Look Up

When creating an entry, ask yourself whether you would be likely as a user to look in the index for that entry.

Examples of some questionable entries:

- Entries starting with terms such as "how" or "why"
- Entries starting with irrelevant terms

  For example, "creating the file" should not be indexed under "creating."

- Commands or widgets, used only in sample programs or examples

  For example, in a book in which an exercise involves creating the buttons "Hello!" and "Adios!" don't include "Hello!" and "Adios!" as index entries.

- Titles of books in a "Recommended Reading" section
- Entries drawn solely from section heads

Select Proper Words for Subjects

The words you select are an abstract of the topic. Choose words that are as descriptive as possible. Using words from the text as subjects of index entries may satisfy readers who know the terminology used in the document. For other readers, provide subjects or cross-references worded so that they can find the desired information without specific prior knowledge.

Arrange Words for Emphasis

Typically, you will make the most important word the first word of the subject. The choice of *most important word* depends upon what you want to stress or what is most important to a reader. For example, if the words you choose to describe a topic are "pixwin background color," the primary entries might be:

    background color, pixwin
    color, pixwin background
    pixwin background color

Be careful with the use of verbs as the main subject of an index entry. General verbs may not be helpful. Be sure the verb corresponds specifically to the task the user wants to accomplish. For example, for a discussion about how to use menu buttons, the proper index entry might be:

    menu buttons, using

Or, if there are additional (secondary) entries, you might format the entry as:

    menu buttons
        default
        using

Assign the Proper Font to the Entry

Keep in mind that certain terms may require different fonts if they are being referred to in different contexts. You also may need to include a word such as "command," "file," or "directory" after such terms to further clarify the entry.

> `quit` command
>
> quit, in contrast to exit

Group Entries

Grouping entries means combining entries that have common first words into primary entries and secondary entries.

Ungrouped Entries	Grouped Entries

SBus, introduction
SBus block diagram
SBus specifications
	SBus ◄———————— Primary entry
	  block diagram ⎫
	  introduction ⎬ Secondary entries
	  specifications ⎭

When selecting a subject to be followed by secondary entries, be careful to group subjects properly. Don't merely select a word or phrase for a subject because it is common to several entries. For example, assume that the following subjects appeared in your document:

> rock, igneous
>
> rock, metamorphic
>
> rock music

To factor out "rock" and create three secondary entries would be wrong. If you analyze the use of "rock" in each entry, you can see that it is used in two different ways.

Wrong	Right

rock
  igneous, 4-2
  metamorphic, 4-18
  music, 12-5
	rock
	  igneous, 4-2
	  metamorphic, 4-18
	rock music 12-5

Create Index Entries for Notes, Cautions, and Warnings

You want a reader to be able to locate the various restrictions in your document. The types of restrictions include:

- Sets of rules
- Value limits (maximums and minimums)
- Incompatibilities between features and options
- Caution and Warning notices

Most of the topics that qualify as restrictions are not stated as such in the text. You must analyze the text to find the restrictions to index. The wording of the subject should describe the nature of the restriction.

In the next example, the correctly worded index entry enables readers who are familiar with the document organization to ignore the entry if they already know the restriction:

> symbolic names, maximum length of

However, the incorrect wording below would require nearly every reader to look up the subject to find the restriction:

> symbolic names, restriction

In many documents, certain restrictions are identified specifically because of their importance. For example, assume the following Caution notice appeared in your document:

Caution – Never turn on or off the system unit while a diskette is in the disk drive. You may damage the diskette.

This restriction should be described in the index and flagged with the word "Caution." The entry might be:

> turning system on or off, Caution notice

Create Index Entries for Acronyms and Abbreviations

Include an acronym or abbreviation in your index if it is unique to your document (or manual set) and not likely to be found in common usage. Many acronyms and abbreviations need not be included in an index. For example, the abbreviations for most units of measure (Btu, in., lbs, and so on) are not good candidates for indexing.

When you include an acronym or abbreviation in an index, follow it with the words (in parentheses) from which it was formed.

> CCP (console command processor), 1-5

Double-post the term by adding an entry for the words that form the acronym or abbreviation, followed by the acronym or abbreviation in parentheses.

> console command processor (CCP), 1-5

Double-Posting Entries

Double-posting means identifying a topic in two different places in an index. For example, a topic that appears as "address switch" and "switch, address" is double-posted in the index. A topic that appears in three places is triple-posted, and so on.

Entry	Double- or Triple-Posted Entries
power indicator	power indicator indicator, power
C shell command interpreter	C shell command interpreter command interpreter, C shell interpreter, C shell command

Be careful of over-indexing with double-posting. Certain entries do not deserve double-posting. For instance, the following example might be acceptable in a document that refers to only a few commands.

Entry	Double-Posted Entries
grep command	grep command command, grep

However, for a manual with several commands, the entries under "command" might grow too numerous. In this case, rather than creating a primary entry of "command" with many secondary entries, index the commands under the command name—do not double-post—and include a cross-reference.

Entries	Double-Posted Entries
cat command grep command history command . .	commands, *See* specific command names

Double-posting increases the number of index entries available to a reader, which broadens the scope of the index. The knowledgable reader is not forced to scan the index for a general entry when seeking a specific topic.

Double-posting has a dramatic effect on usability; it is an essential technique for creating a high-quality index. Try to double-post entries for all key concepts and important terminology.

Keep in mind, however, that there is a fundamental tradeoff involved in double-posting an index. While an extensively double-posted index provides a denser, more comprehensive view of a document's topics, it also significantly increases your indexing workload. Be sure to include enough time in your schedule for double-posting your index.

Creating "See" and "See Also" References

You cross-reference index entries by creating "See" and "See also" references.

When to Use "See" and "See Also" References

Use a "See" reference when you have so many secondary entries that repeating them would be unreasonable.

> configuration, *See* measurement configuration
>
> .
>
> .
>
> .
>
> measurement configuration
> > applying storage thresholds
> > calculating line speeds
> > defining data fields
> > defining entities

Use a "See" reference to send readers from a broad category to a more specific category. The next example is valid only if there are several secondary entries under "display thresholds," "exception thresholds," and "storage thresholds." Otherwise, you would double-post.

> thresholds, *See* display thresholds; exception thresholds; storage
> > thresholds

Use a "See" reference to direct a reader from a term not used in the document to a term that is used as an index entry.

> cars, *See* automobiles

Consider using a "See also" reference to direct a reader to related information at another index entry. (Depending upon how your index is structured, you might also use a "See also" cross-reference from a specific category to a general one.)

> dBASE, 37
> > *See also* database applications

Use a "See also" reference to avoid fourth-level entries.

> performance database
> > backing up data in
> > deleting
> > updating
> > *See also* update, performance database
> > > .
> > > .
> > > .

> update, performance database
> > displaying status
> > starting
> > automatic
> > manual
> > stopping

How to Use "See" and "See Also" References

Place "See" references on the same line as the entry.

> UNIX, *See* operating system

Place "See also" references immediately below the entry on which they are based.

> exception conditions
> > *See also* panel indicators
> > sense command, 5-22
> > status byte, 2-4
> > > *See also* PSW
> > store violation, 3-7

Some noun modifiers (such as "data" and "file") are ubiquitous in the computer industry. If you have several long and complicated entries that start with the same word, readers might not look far enough to find a given topic. In this case, use a "See also" reference to help a reader.

> data
> > *See also* data files; data records
> > collecting
> > purging

Never use a "See" reference with an entry that has a page number.

> *Wrong:*

> structured files, 7-3
>   *See* files, structured

Don't use unnecessary "See" references. If you can reasonably double-post an entry, do so. Readers have every right to be annoyed if you send them searching through an index just for one or two page numbers.

Wrong	Right
command objects, *See* objects	command objects, 5-2, 5-8
.	.
.	.
.	.
objects, 5-2, 5-8	objects, 5-2, 5-8

In particular, don't send readers from a specific entry to a general entry, under which they must then search for the specific entry. However, be careful that you don't exclude general information that should be included under the specific entry as well. In the following example, "changing report attributes" must be included under the entries for specific reports, because a user might not look at the general entry.

Wrong	Right
forecast report, *See* reporting	forecast report, 3-67 changing report attributes, 3-122
.	.
.	.
.	.
reporting	reporting
automatic, 2-33, 3-174	automatic, 2-33, 3-174
changing report attributes, 3-122	changing report attributes, 3-122
forecast reports, 3-67	forecast reports, 3-67
predefined reports, 3-71	predefined reports, 3-71

Don't include a page number with a "See also" reference.

> *Wrong:*

> structured files, 7-3
>   *See also* chaotic files, 8-4

Don't use a "See also" reference to send a reader to a duplicate (double-posted) entry in an index.

> *Wrong:*

> entry-sequenced files, 7-3
>> *See also* files, entry-sequenced

>> .

>> .

>> .

> files, entry-sequenced, 7-3

Make sure that a "See" or "See also" reference repeats the exact wording of the entry to which it refers.

Wrong	Right
database, *See* PDB	database, *See* performance database (PDB)
.	.
.	.
.	.
performance database (PDB)	performance database (PDB)

Avoiding Indexing Problems

This section explains some established rules for indexing. If you disregard them, you will confuse or annoy your reader, and appear incompetent to any reader who is knowledgable about indexing.

Don't Use a Two-Level Entry for a Single Topic

If you can use the primary entry alone, do so. A primary term with only one secondary term should be on a single text line. If you feel that the primary entry alone is misleading, rewrite it.

Wrong	Right

optimization routines
    use of, 38
	optimization routines, 38
	    or
	optimization routines, use of, 38

Don't Use an Adjective Alone as a Primary Entry

Adjectives without related nouns do not provide enough information for a reader.

Wrong	Right
implicit	implicit commands
`logoff` command, 6-4	`logoff`, 6-4
`open` command, 6-1	`open`, 6-1
`wait` command, 6-6	`wait`, 6-6

This rule applies (emphatically) to noun modifiers—that is, nouns that are being used as adjectives. This rule eliminates awkward, confusing constructions in which the primary entry is a noun relative to some secondary entries and an adjective relative to others.

Wrong	Right
data	data
collecting, 81	collecting, 81
files, 90	purging, 62
purging, 62	data files, 90
records, 47	data records, 47
.	.
.	.
.	.
`wait`	`wait` command, 29
command, 29	`wait` parameter, 33
parameter, 33	

Don't Use an Overly General Primary Entry

Generally, if a primary entry is followed by half a page or so of secondary entries, either the primary entry is too broad or you are over-indexing. For example, in a printer manual, the primary entry "printer" is too broad to be indexed as a term.

In a reference manual containing mostly commands, a primary entry of "commands" followed by a long list of commands is probably not helpful to a reader. Rather, each command should be indexed in its proper alphabetical place.

Read Me First!

If you feel that it is necessary or helpful, use "commands" plus a "See" reference to send a reader to alternate methods of locating a given command.

Not Preferred	Preferred

commands
   alias, 14
   at, 19
   batch, 23
 	
   .
   .
   .
 	
   ypmatch, 132
   ypwhich, 134
   zcat, 135
	(no entry at all, if most of the document describes commands)
	
	or
	
	commands, *See* individual commands by name
	
	or
	
	commands, summary of, 18

Don't Over-Index

Don't provide so many entries that they get in a reader's way. For example, in a reference manual containing many commands or utilities, you might be tempted to index the subheadings under each command. This often results in over-indexing, as shown below.

Not Preferred	Preferred

ast command
   attributes, 42
   syntax, 33
ast_process command
   attributes, 49
   syntax, 44
ast_subvolume command
   attributes, 55
   syntax, 51
	ast command, 33, 42
	ast_process command, 44, 49
	ast_subvolume command, 51, 55

Over-indexing also occurs if you create several secondary entries under a primary entry when all entries are on the same page.

Not Preferred	Preferred

input devices
   buttons, 167
   dials, 167
   digitizer, 167
   scanner, 167
	input devices, 167

Don't provide two adjacent entries that are very similar. The test: If you omit an entry, can a reader still find the right place in the document?

Not Preferred	Preferred
`delete_file` command, 41 deleting a file, 41	`delete_file` command, 41

Don't Under-Index

Some kinds of under-indexing are very obvious, as they do not provide enough specific information to be useful to a reader.

Not Preferred	Preferred

reports, 31–39, 77	reports
	    exporting, 77
	    generating, 34
	    preformatting, 33
	    specifying format, 36–39
	    types of, 31–33

Other types of under-indexing aren't obvious, except to a reader. It is especially important to index *concepts*, not just the terms that appear in the document.

Not Preferred	Preferred
`archive` command, 77	`archive` command, 77 . . . backing up data to tape, 77 . . . tape backups, 77

Don't Alphabetize Subentries by Beginning Articles, Conjunctions, or Prepositions

Use only the key term when alphabetizing entries. This enables a reader to focus on the key term in the entry.

Wrong	Right
transformation 　　matrix representation, 16 　　of raster images, 18 　　process, 14 　　refresh buffer, 3	transformation 　　matrix representation, 16 　　process, 14 　　of raster images, 18 　　refresh buffer, 3

Don't Alphabetize by Symbol for Path Names, File Names, File Prefixes, or Variables

For path, file, or variable entries that begin with a symbol, alphabetize these entries by the first letter of the first word following the symbol.

Not Preferred	Preferred

Symbols
`_config`
`/etc/uucp/Limits`
`.info`
`$PATH`
 	
E
error reporting
external files
	C
	cancel command
	`_config`
	Create menu
	
	E
	error reporting
	`/etc/uucp/Limits`
	external files
	
	I
	ID numbers
	`.info`
	
	P
	`$PATH`
	primary numbers

Don't Sort Subentries by a Word That Isn't the Key Term

Avoid beginning a subentry with a word that isn't the key term in the subentry. To help a reader, whenever possible you should reword the subentry so that the key term, rather than an irrelevant introductory word, appears at the beginning of the subentry.

Wrong	Right

accounting
    software for, 11
    summary of commands, 38
addressing
    issues for virtual networks, 34
    naming conventions, 52
	accounting
	    command summary, 38
	    software for, 11
	addressing
	    naming conventions, 52
	    virtual network issues, 34

Don't Capitalize Words Without a Reason

Avoid capitalizing words except proper nouns and acronyms that are necessarily capitalized.

Wrong	Right
Data files	data files
pid (program ID number)	PID (program ID) number
ethernet	Ethernet

Editing an Index

While creating the first draft of your index, you probably concentrated mostly on the individual entries and their secondary entries. While editing the index, you are concerned with the index as a whole.

Editing an index may require that you create or delete entries, combine or split up entries, and regroup or reword entries. In a sense, editing an index is not very different from editing the document. Namely, you verify that all necessary material is included, that it is in the intended order, and that it is error-free.

Remember that you are reading an index in an abnormal way; that is, you are reading it from start to finish. Normally, your readers go directly to the word or phrase they hope to find. Because you are reading an index this way, you may think that many entries are not necessary or are redundant. For some entries, this may be true, but to delete many entries on that basis alone is risky. Unless your analysis of the topic was wrong when you created the entry, you probably had a specific reason for making the entry.

Check the Spelling

Many publishing systems don't check the spelling in the embedded index entries when the spelling checker is run on the body of the document. For this reason, you should always carefully proofread and run the spelling checker on index entries to catch spelling and typographical errors.

Check the Levels of Secondary Entries

Check the levels of secondary entries so that proper indentation shows the relationship of one entry to the preceding one. See "Nested Entries" on page 151.

Check for Differences in Wording

Check the subjects to determine whether slight variations of wording are intentional or whether you should use only one wording. If there are valid subjects that differ only slightly in wording, examine them to be sure that your readers are able to recognize the differences; you may have to reword the subjects to make the differences apparent.

Many times you will discover after creating the index that you have used inconsistent terminology in the document. This is a good time to check for consistency and make any necessary corrections, even though it means taking a little more time.

Check for Misused Singular and Plural Forms

Check the entries for the misuse of singular and plural forms. Usually, only one form of a subject is justified; therefore, you should combine secondary entries under one subject. Using both forms of a subject (such as "data set" and "data sets") usually causes errors. Several other entries and their subsequent secondary entries may intervene between the singular and plural forms of a subject. A reader should not have to check the index for both forms.

Wrong	Right
data set	data sets
input	address
output	area
data set address	format of
data set area	input
data sets	output
format of	table of
table of	

Check for Redundant Secondary Entries

Check main entries that are followed by secondary entries having the same page reference.

In many cases, you can eliminate the secondary entries because a reader will find all the information on one page. Redundant secondary entries often occur when indexing items in a table. See "Don't Over-Index" on page 167.

Wrong	Right

data sets
    format of, 2-7
    table of, 2-7
	data sets, 2-7

Check for Effective Double-Posting

Check that all meaningful variations of a subject's wording appear in an index. See "Group Entries" on page 159.

Check Secondary Entries for Possible Primary Entries

Check each secondary entry to see if it should also appear as a primary entry. If it should, verify that it exists as such or create the primary entry and insert it in the proper place.

Check for Possible Rearrangement of Secondary Entries

Check if secondary entries should be rearranged to stress a certain point. In this example, all three secondary entries should probably be in the same form. The form depends on what you want to stress.

Wrong	Right

window system
    colors, changing, 8-11
    icon, moving, 4-22
    saving properties, 8-15
	window system
	    colors, changing, 8-11
	    icon, moving, 4-22
	    properties, saving, 8-15

Check for Appropriately Combined Secondary Entries

Review an index to make sure that you have combined relevant entries.

Wrong	Right

DeskSet
    selection protocol, 2-4
DeskSet atoms, 4-8
DeskSet Drag and Drop atoms, 4-4
DeskSet drag and drop handshaking, 4-2
deskset integration
    why do it, 1-2
	DeskSet
	    atoms, 4-8
	    drag and drop
	        atoms, 4-4
	        handshaking, 4-2
	    integration, 1-2
	    selection protocol, 2-4

Check for Secondary Entries Under More Than One Subject

Check for secondary entries that should be arranged under one subject rather than appearing under several. Such division of secondary entries is usually the result of misused "See also" references.

Wrong	Right

find function
    See also search function
    examples, 8-22
    use of, 8-15
    variables, 8-18
.
.
.
search function
    dialog box, 8-9
    and replace function, 8-21
	find function
	    dialog box, 8-9
	    examples, 8-22
	    and replace function, 8-21
	    use of, 8-15
	    variables, 8-18
	.
	.
	.
	search function, *See* find function

9

Check for Secondary Entries When Using a Combined Term Separately

Check for and move a secondary entry if you included the combined term as a separate entry.

In the next example, the entries starting with "database" under the "classing engine" main entry belong under the "classing engine database" main entry.

Wrong	Right

classing engine
  adding a new file type, 6-6
  attributes, 6-4
  database, accessing, 6-7
  database, converting, 6-8
  database, reading, 6-8
  interactive modification, 6-5
  mapping function, 6-3
classing engine database
  location of, 6-7
  network, 6-9
	classing engine
	  adding a new file type, 6-6
	  attributes, 6-4
	  interactive modification, 6-5
	  mapping function, 6-3
	classing engine database
	  accessing, 6-7
	  converting, 6-8
	  location of, 6-7
	  network, 6-9
	  reading, 6-8

Check the Number of Page References for Entries

Depending upon the complexity of your material, each index entry should have no more than two to four page references. If an entry has more than two to four page references, see if you can create secondary and tertiary entries to reduce the number of page references.

Wrong	Right

block diagram, 21, 28, 33, 37	block diagram
	  attribute generator, 33
	  frame buffer, 37
	  front-end processor, 28
	  SBus adapter, 21

Read Me First!

Check the Proper Topic Cross-References

Check that the page references for each occurrence of a topic are the same and that they appear in each place. In the example, a reader looking up "operator messages" would not be aware of all the other places where information exists. Create secondary entries under "operator messages" and give your readers the same information they would have found had they looked up "messages."

Wrong	Right
messages	messages
from operator, 2-34	from operator, 2-34
to operator, 2-15, 3-7	to operator, 2-15, 3-7
to programmer, 5-12	to programmer, 5-12
.	.
.	.
.	.
operator messages, 2-34, 3-7	operator messages, 2-34, 3-7
.	from operator, 2-34
.	to operator, 2-15, 3-7
.	to programmer, 5-12

Check the Secondary Entries Under Various Forms of One Topic

Check that the number of secondary entries under various forms of the same topic are all the same. In the example, "attention key" should appear after the "terminal, communications" entry so that readers are aware of the information regardless of how they look it up.

Wrong	Right
communications terminal	communications terminal
attention key, 4-16	attention key, 4-16
polling character, 4-11	polling character, 4-11
READY indicator, 4-10	READY indicator, 4-10
.	.
.	.
.	.
terminal, communications	terminal, communications
polling character, 4-11	attention key, 4-16
READY indicator, 4-10	polling character, 4-11
	READY indicator, 4-10

Check the "See" and "See Also" References

Check that each "See" reference refers to an entry with secondary entries. Read "Creating "See" and "See Also" References" on page 162.

Check the Size of the Index

After you have edited the index, compare the size of the index with the size of the document. Although the index size is not an indication of its quality, an index that is too small for the size of the document should make you suspicious; it might indicate serious omissions.

A minimum length for an index should be one page of index entries for every 20 pages of text, or about one index entry for every 100 words of text. This would be considered a "5 percent" index. For dense technical material; however, this guideline is too low. A dense technical manual should have one page of index entries for every 10 pages of text, which would be considered a "10 percent" index.

If you check the length of your index by page count (rather than by word count), do not count text pages that contain any of the following if they occupy more than about two-thirds of a page:

- Flowcharts
- Figures
- Code examples
- Front matter (title page, contents, and so on)
- Blank space longer than three-quarters of a page
- Glossary or bibliography

If the index falls below the guidelines, check that all topics in the document are entered in the index.

Correct Bad Page and Column Breaks

One form of bad page break results when a primary entry with multiple secondary entries (or even tertiary entries) breaks in the middle at the foot of the last column on a right page. The first column on the following page begins with an indented (secondary or tertiary) entry. Bad page breaks cause problems for a reader, who must look back to the previous page to find the primary entry.

Correct bad page breaks by repeating the primary entry above the carried-over secondary entry followed by the word continued in italics and surrounded by parentheses. Don't repeat the page numbers, if included, from the previous primary or secondary entry. In the example, the primary entry "menus" includes a page range, but the page range is not repeated on the next page.

menus, 3–22	menus (*continued*)
general navigation, 3	Graphics, 16
Edit, 8	Special, 20
File, 10	Table, 21
Format, 12	View, 22

In the rare case where this type of bad break occurs on a secondary entry with multiple tertiary entries, repeat the primary entry at the top of the column. Then, repeat the secondary entry, indented, followed by the word "continued." Do not include the word "continued" after the primary entry.

graphical user interface	graphical user interface
menus	menus (*continued*)
general navigation, 3	Graphics, 16
Edit, 8	Special, 20
File, 10	Table, 21
Format, 12	View, 22

A single primary entry at the beginning of an alphabetic section should not stand at the bottom of a column. Force the alphabetic character to the top of the next column, carrying the single primary entry along with it.

Likewise, don't leave a single line at the end of an alphabetic section at the top of a column. Force a column break one or two lines before the widowed line.

A Global Index

The type of index most writers work with is the "back-of-the-book" variety. A *global index* combines the back-of-the-book indexes from all the books in a set. A global index is a valuable information retrieval device for a reader who is not intimately familiar with all the books in a set. A global index provides a single place where readers can find the information they seek without having to look through several individual indexes.

Formatting a Global Index

In a global index, merely referring a reader to page numbers is insufficient. Because a global index combines the indexes from several books in a set, a reader also needs to know the book in the set to which the reference applies. For this reason, a global index requires a special page numbering style. One method is to use a four-letter abbreviation for an entry's book title, with a running footer that provides a legend on each index page for the abbreviations. If running such a footer is not possible or desirable, put a legend for abbreviations at the beginning of the index.

Editing a Global Index

Because of its size and complexity, a global index is by far the most difficult type of index to create properly. It is not sufficient just to combine the indexes from several books and assume that, if the previous back-of-the-book indexes were correct, a global index will also be correct.

When combining indexes to make a global index, the indexer must edit the global index for most of the indexing mistakes described under "Editing an Index." Specifically, the indexer must check for:

- Levels of secondary entries
- Differences in wording
- Misuse of singular and plural forms
- Meaningful variations (double-posting) of a subject's wording
- Possible rearrangement of secondary entries
- Bad page and column breaks

Many of these mistakes may creep into a global index even though they may not have been in the original indexes. These mistakes happen when common terms in different indexes are combined, slightly different terminology is used in different books, and different indexing choices have been applied in each book.

There are two ways to fix the problems that result from creating a global index:

- Edit the index entries in the original text and re-create the index.
- Edit the global index and leave the index entries as they are in the original text.

Recommended Reading

A≡

This appendix contains some titles on general and technical writing and editing, as well as books primarily for technical writers in the computer industry.

Recommendations cover the following categories:

- Writing standards
- Editing standards
- Project management
- Reference books
- Indexing
- Platform style guides
- Legal issues
- Internationalization and localization
- User interfaces
- On-line publishing
- Typography
- Graphics and illustration
- Desktop publishing
- Printing
- Info mapping
- Standard Generalized Markup Language (SGML)
- World Wide Web (WWW)

A

Writing Standards

Barnum, Carol M., and Saul Carliner. *Techniques for Technical Communicators*. New York: Macmillan, 1993.

Barrett, Edward, ed. *Text, ConText, and HyperText: Writing With and For the Computer*. Cambridge, Mass.: MIT Press, 1988.

Barzun, Jacques. *Simple & Direct: A Rhetoric for Writers*. Rev. ed. Chicago: University of Chicago Press, 1994.

Bly, Robert, and Gary Blake. *Technical Writing Structure, Standards and Style*. New York: McGraw-Hill, 1982.

Brockmann, R. John. *Writing Better Computer User Documentation: From Paper to Online*. New York: John Wiley & Sons, 1986.

Brogan, John A. *Clear Technical Writing*. New York: McGraw-Hill, 1973.

Brooks, Brian S. *Working With Words*. 2d ed. New York: St. Martin's Press, 1993.

Brusaw, Charles T. *Handbook of Technical Writing*. 4th ed. New York: St. Martin's Press, 1993.

Burnett, Rebecca E. *Technical Communication*. 3d ed. Belmont, Calif.: Wadsworth Publishing Co., 1994.

Copperud, Roy H. *American Usage and Style, the Consensus*. New York: Van Nostrand Reinhold, 1980.

Denton, Lynn, and Jody Kelly. *Designing, Writing, and Producing Computer Documentation*. New York: McGraw-Hill, 1992.

Dupre, Lyn. *Bugs in Writing: A Guide to Debugging Your Prose*. Reading, Mass.: Addison-Wesley, 1995.

Eisenberg, Anne. *Writing Well for the Technical Professions*. New York: Harper & Row, 1989.

Flesch, Rudolf. *The Art of Readable Writing*. New York: Macmillan, 1986.

Flesch, Rudolf, and A.H. Lass. *A New Guide to Better Writing*. New York: Warner Books, 1989.

Lutz, William. *Doublespeak*. 1st ed. New York: Harper & Row, 1989.

Perry, Carol Rosenblum. *The Fine Art of Technical Writing*, 1st ed. Hillsboro, Oreg.: Blue Heron Publishing, 1991.

Price, Jonathan. *How to Write a Computer Manual: A Handbook of Software Documentation*. Menlo Park, Calif.: Benjamin/Cummings Publishing Co., 1984.

Sides, Charles H. *How to Write & Present Technical Information*. 2d ed. Phoenix, Ariz.: Oryx Press, 1991.

Strunk, William, Jr., and E. B. White. *Elements of Style*. 3d ed. New York: Macmillan, 1979.

Tracz, Richard Francis. *Dr. Grammar's Writes From Wrongs*. New York: Vintage Books, 1991.

Weiss, Edmond H. *How to Write a Usable User Manual*. Philadelphia: ISI Press, 1985.

Woolever, Kristen R., and Helen M. Loeb. *Writing for the Computer Industry*. Englewood Cliffs, N.J.: Prentice Hall, 1994.

Zinsser, William. *On Writing Well: An Informal Guide to Writing Nonfiction*. 5th ed. New York: Harper Perennial, 1994.

Editing Standards

Bush, Donald W., and Charles P. Campbell. *How to Edit Technical Documents*. Phoenix, Ariz.: Oryx Press, 1995.

Gordon, Karen Elizabeth. *The Deluxe Transitive Vampire: The Ultimate Handbook of Grammar for the Innocent, the Eager, and the Doomed*. 1st ed. New York: Pantheon Books, 1993.

Gordon, Karen Elizabeth. *The Well-Tempered Sentence, A Punctuation Handbook for the Innocent, the Eager, and the Doomed*. Revised and expanded. New York: Ticknor & Fields, 1993.

Judd, Karen. *Copyediting, a Practical Guide*. 2d ed. Los Altos, Calif.: Crisp Publications, 1990.

Perdue, Lewis. *The High Technology Editorial Guide and Stylebook*. Macintosh or PC ed. Homewood, Ill.: Business One Irwin, 1991.

Ross-Larson, Bruce. *Edit Yourself*. New York: W. W. Norton & Co., 1982.

Rude, Carolyn D. *Technical Editing*. Belmont, Calif.: Wadsworth Publishing, 1991.

Samson, Donald C., Jr. *Editing Technical Writing*. New York: Oxford University Press, 1993.

Tarutz, Judith A. *Technical Editing: The Practical Guide for Editors and Writers*. Reading, Mass.: Addison-Wesley, 1992.

Venolia, Jan. *Rewrite Right!* Berkeley, Calif.: Ten Speed Press/Periwinkle Press, 1987.

A

Project Management

Brooks, Frederick P. *The Mythical Man-Month: Essays on Software Engineering*. Anniversary ed. Reading, Mass.: Addison-Wesley, 1995.

Caird, Helen G. *Publications Cost Management*. Anthology Series No. 3. Washington, D.C.: Society for Technical Communication, May 1975.

DeMarco, Tom. *Controlling Software Projects: Management, Measurement & Estimation*. New York: Yourdon Press, 1982.

Dreger, J. Brian. *Project Management: Effective Scheduling*. New York: Van Nostrand Reinhold, 1992.

Hackos, JoAnn T. *Managing Your Documentation Projects*. New York: John Wiley & Sons, 1994.

Humphrey, Watts S. *Managing the Software Process*. Reading, Mass.: Addison-Wesley, 1989.

Kerzner, Harold. *Project Management: A Systems Approach to Planning, Scheduling, and Controlling*. 5th ed. New York: Van Nostrand Reinhold, 1995.

Nicholas, John M. *Managing Business and Engineering Projects: Concepts and Implementation*. Englewood Cliffs, N.J.: Prentice Hall, 1990.

Sandra Pakin and Associates, Inc. *Documentation Development Methodology: Techniques for Improved Communications*. Englewood Cliffs, N.J.: Prentice Hall, 1984.

Roman, Daniel D. *Managing Projects: A Systems Approach*. New York: Elsevier, 1986.

Zells, Lois. *Managing Software Projects: Selecting and Using PC-Based Project Management Systems*. Wellesley, Mass.: QED Information Sciences, 1990.

Reference Books

The Chicago Manual of Style. 14th ed. Chicago: University of Chicago Press, 1993.

IBM Dictionary of Computing. 10th ed. New York: McGraw-Hill, 1993.

IEEE Standard Dictionary of Electrical and Electronics Terms. 5th ed. New York: Institute of Electrical and Electronics Engineers, Inc., 1993.

McGraw-Hill Dictionary of Scientific and Technical Terms. 5th ed. New York: McGraw-Hill, 1993.

Markus, John. *McGraw-Hill Electronics Dictionary*. 5th ed. New York: McGraw-Hill, 1994.

Merriam-Webster's Collegiate Dictionary. 10th ed. Springfield, Mass.: Merriam-Webster, 1995.

Merriam-Webster's Collegiate Thesaurus. Springfield, Mass.: Merriam-Webster, 1993.

Microsoft Press Computer Dictionary. 2d ed. Redmond, Wash.: Microsoft Press, 1994.

The New York Public Library Writer's Guide to Style and Usage. 1st ed. New York: Harper Collins, 1994.

The Random House Dictionary of the English Language. 2d ed. New York: Random House, 1987.

Raymond, Eric S., ed. *The New Hacker's Dictionary.* 2d ed. Cambridge, Mass.: MIT Press, 1993.

Sabin, William A. *The Gregg Reference Manual.* 6th ed. New York: Gregg Division/McGraw-Hill, 1985.

Webster's Third New International Dictionary. Springfield, Mass.: Merriam-Webster, 1993.

Williams, Robin, and Steve Cummings. *Jargon: An Informal Dictionary of Computer Terms.* Berkeley, Calif.: Peachpit Press, 1993.

Words into Type. 3d ed. Based on studies by Marjorie E. Skillin, Robert M. Gay, and other authorities. Englewood Cliffs, N.J.: Prentice Hall, 1974.

Xerox Publishing Standards: A Manual of Style and Design. New York: Watson-Guptill Publications, Inc., 1988.

Indexing

Bonura, Larry. *The Art of Indexing.* New York: John Wiley & Sons, 1994.

Mulvany, Nancy C. *Indexing Books.* Chicago: University of Chicago Press, 1994.

Wellisch, Hans H. *Indexing From A to Z.* Bronx, N.Y.: H.W. Wilson, 1991.

Platform Style Guides

Apple Computer, Inc. *Macintosh Human Interface Guidelines.* Reading, Mass.: Addison-Wesley, 1992.

Commodore-Amiga, Inc. *Amiga User Interface Style Guide.* Reading, Mass.: Addison-Wesley, 1991.

GO Corporation. *PenPoint User Interface Design Reference*. Reading, Mass.: Addison-Wesley, 1992.

Martin, James. *Systems Application Architecture: Common Programming Interface*. Englewood Cliffs, N.J.: PTR Prentice Hall, 1993.

NeXTSTEP User Interface Guidelines, Release 3. NeXT Computer, Inc., Reading, Mass.: Addison-Wesley, 1992.

Object-Oriented Interface Design: IBM Common User Access Guidelines. 1st ed. Carmel, Ind.: Que, 1992.

OSF/Motif Style Guide: Revision 1.2 (for OSF/Motif Release 1.2). Englewood Cliffs, N.J.: PTR Prentice Hall, 1993.

Microsoft Corporation. *The GUI Guide: International Terminology for the Windows Interface*. European ed. Redmond, Wash.: Microsoft Press, 1993.

Microsoft Corporation. *The Windows Interface: An Application Design Guide*. Redmond, Wash.: Microsoft Press, 1992.

Sun Microsystems, Inc. *OPEN LOOK Graphical User Interface Application Style Guidelines*. Reading, Mass.: Addison-Wesley, 1989.

Sun Microsystems, Inc. *OPEN LOOK Graphical User Interface Functional Specification*. Reading, Mass.: Addison-Wesley, 1989.

Legal Issues

Foster, Frank H. *Patents, Copyrights, and Trademarks*. 2d ed. New York: John Wiley & Sons, 1993.

Rose, Lance. *NetLaw: Your Rights in the Online World*. New York: Osborne/McGraw-Hill, 1995.

Strong, William S. *The Copyright Book*. Cambridge, Mass.: MIT Press, 1981.

Internationalization and Localization

Carter, Daniel. *Writing Localizable Software for the Macintosh*. Reading, Mass.: Addison-Wesley, 1992.

Fernandes, Tony. *Global Interface Design*. Cambridge, Mass.: AP Professional, 1995.

Hoft, Nancy L. *International Technical Communication: How to Export Information about High Technology*. New York: John Wiley & Sons, 1995.

Kennelly, Cynthia Hartman. *Digital Guide to Developing International Software.* Corporate User Publications Group/Digital Equipment Corporation. Bedford, Mass.: Digital Press, 1991.

Taylor, Dave. *Global Software: Developing Applications for the International Market.* New York: Springer-Verlag, 1992.

Tuthill, Bill. *Solaris International Developer's Guide.* Mountain View, Calif.: SunSoft Press, 1993.

Uren, Emmanuel, Robert Howard, and Tiziana Perinotti. *Software Internationalization and Localization: An Introduction.* New York: Van Nostrand Reinhold, 1993.

User Interfaces

Galitz, Wilbert O. *User-Interface Screen Design.* Boston: QED Publishing Group, 1993.

Hix, Deborah, and H. Rex Hartson. *Developing User Interfaces: Ensuring Usability Through Product & Process.* New York: John Wiley & Sons, 1993.

Laurel, Brenda. *The Art of Human-Computer Interface Design.* Reading, Mass.: Addison-Wesley, 1990.

On-line Publishing

Boggan, Scott, David Farkas, and Joe Welinske. *Developing Online Help for Windows.* 1st ed. Carmel, Ind.: Sams Publishing, 1993.

Horton, William K. *Designing and Writing Online Documentation: Hypermedia for Self-Supporting Products.* 2d ed. New York: John Wiley & Sons, 1994.

Stovall, James Glen. *On-line Editing.* Northport, Ala.: Vision Press, 1994.

Typography

Bringhurst, Robert. *Elements of Typographic Style.* 1st ed. Point Roberts, Wash.: Hartley & Marks, 1992.

Haley, Allan. *ABC's of Type.* New York: Watson-Guptill Publications, Inc., 1990.

Rehe, Rolf F. *Typography: How to Make It Most Legible.* 4th rev. ed. Carmel, Ind.: Design Research International, 1981.

Spiekermann, Erik, and E. M. Ginger. *Stop Stealing Sheep & Find Out How Type Works*. Mountain View, Calif.: Adobe Press, 1993.

Williams, Robin. *The Non-Designer's Design Book: Design and Typographic Principles for the Visual Novice*. Berkeley, Calif.: Peachpit Press, 1994.

Graphics and Illustration

American Institute of Graphic Arts. *Symbol Signs: The System of Passenger/Pedestrian Oriented Symbols Developed for the U.S. Department of Transportation*. New York: Hastings House, 1981.

Craig, James. *Working With Graphic Designers*. New York: MIS Watson-Guptill Publications, Inc., 1989.

Gosney, Michael, and Linnea Dayton. *The Desktop Color Book: A Verbum Guide*. 2d ed. New York: MIS Press, 1995.

Hartley, James. *Designing Instructional Text*. 3d ed. London: Kogan Page; East Brunswick, N.J.: Nichols, 1994.

Horton, William K. *The Icon Book: Visual Symbols for Computer Systems and Documentation*. New York: John Wiley & Sons, 1994.

Horton, William K. *Illustrating Computer Documentation: The Art of Presenting Information Graphically on Paper and Online*. New York: John Wiley & Sons, 1991.

Marcus, Aaron. *Graphic Design for Electronic Documents and User Interfaces*. New York: ACM Press; Reading, Mass.: Addison-Wesley, 1992.

Murray, James D., and William vanRyper. *Encyclopedia of Graphics File Formats*. 1st ed. Sebastopol, Calif.: O'Reilly & Associates, 1994.

Norman, Donald A. *The Design of Everyday Things*. 1st Doubleday/Currency ed. New York: Doubleday, 1990.

Ota, Yukio. *Pictogram Design*. Tokyo: Kashiwashobo, 1987.

Pfeiffer, Katherine Shelly. *Word for Windows Design Companion*. 2d ed. Chapel Hill, N.C.: Ventana Press, 1994.

Pocket Pal: A Graphic Arts Production Handbook. New York: International Paper Co., 1988.

Tufte, Edward R. *Envisioning Information*. Cheshire, Conn.: Graphics Press, 1990.

Tufte, Edward R. *The Visual Display of Quantitative Information*. Cheshire, Conn.: Graphics Press, 1983.

White, Jan V. *Graphic Design for the Electronic Age*. New York: Watson-Guptill Publications, Inc., 1988.

Williamson, Hugh Albert Fordyce. *Methods of Book Design: The Practice of an Industrial Craft*. 3d ed. New Haven, Conn.: Yale University Press, 1983.

Desktop Publishing

Kramer, Felix, and Maggie Lovaas. *Desktop Publishing Success*. Homewood, Ill.: Business One Irwin, 1991.

Lichty, Tom. *Design Principles for Desktop Publishers*. 2d ed. Belmont, Calif.: Wadsworth Publishing Co., 1994.

Printing

Adams, J. Michael. *Printing Technology*. 3d ed. Albany, N.Y.: Delmar Publishers, 1988.

Beach, Mark. *Getting It Printed*. Rev. ed. Cincinnati: North Light Books, 1993.

Info Mapping

Duffy, Thomas M., and Robert Waller, eds. *Designing Usable Texts*. Orlando: Academic Press, 1985.

Horn, Robert E. *Mapping Hypertext: The Analysis, Organization, and Display of Knowledge for the Next Generation of On-line Text and Graphics*. Lexington, Mass.: Lexington Institute, 1989.

Wycoff, Joyce. *Mindmapping: Your Personal Guide to Exploring Creativity and Problem-solving*. New York: Berkley Books, 1991.

Standard Generalized Markup Language (SGML)

Bryan, Martin. *SGML: An Author's Guide to the Standard Generalized Markup Language*. Wokingham, England; Reading, Mass.: Addison-Wesley, 1988.

Goldfarb, Charles F. *The SGML Handbook*. Edited by Yuri Rubinsky. Oxford: Clarendon Press; Oxford and New York: Oxford University Press, 1990.

Van Herwijnen, Eric. *Practical SGML*. 2d ed. Boston: Kluwer Academic Publishers, 1994.

≡ A

World Wide Web (WWW)

Aronson, Larry. *HTML Manual of Style*. Emeryville, Calif.: Ziff-Davis Press, 1994.

December, John, and Neil Randall. *The World Wide Web Unleashed*. 1st ed. Carmel, Ind.: Sams Publishing, 1994.

Graham, Ian S. *The HTML Sourcebook*. New York: John Wiley & Sons, 1995.

Lemay, Laura. *Teach Yourself Web Publishing With HTML in a Week*. Carmel, Ind.: Sams Publishing, 1995.

Liu, Cricket, Jerry Peek, Russ Jones, Bryan Buss, and Adrian Nye. *Managing Internet Information Services: World Wide Web, Gopher, FTP, and More*. Sebastopol, Calif.: O'Reilly & Associates, 1994.

Morris, Mary E.S. *HTML for Fun and Profit*. New Jersey: SunSoft Press/Prentice Hall, 1995.

Pfaffenberger, Bryan. *World Wide Web Bible*. New York: MIS Press, 1995.

Read Me First!

Developing a Publications Department

B≡

As a member of a publications department, your charter is to develop, write, edit, validate, and publish documentation that supports the information needs of your customers.

This appendix provides guidance to help you meet the goals of that charter by giving you information on aspects of publications departments ranging from staffing concerns to technical review procedures. It is primarily intended for companies undergoing rapid growth in their documentation requirements. While most publications-related issues are covered, this appendix does not deal with general management issues such as hiring or personnel reviews.

Topics discussed include how to:

- Establish and justify a documentation department
- Staff your department and determine responsibilities
- Estimate task time and develop a project schedule
- Develop writing, editing, and illustration processes
- Determine production and printing processes

Note – This appendix explains how the publications department fits into a software computer company's organization as an example, so you may have to modify some of the recommended processes and procedures to match your own situation.

For a list of books that cover the topic of management issues in more detail than can be provided in this appendix, see the section "Project Management" in Appendix A, "Recommended Reading."

≡ B

Establishing a Publications Department

The documentation presence in a company usually begins with a few people producing written material to accompany products. Publications departments can range from a single permanent publications manager working solely with outside contractors to a department featuring several writing, illustration, and production groups. Table B-1 describes the maturity levels of documentation organizations and their goals at each level.[1]

Use this table to see where your department fits on the continuum. When analyzing your organization, judge its performance as a whole over a long period of time. Although your organization may exhibit some features of a particular level, one instance does not define your organization as having achieved that level of maturity.

Table B-1   Process Maturity Levels of Documentation Organizations

Level	Description	Publications Project Management	Transition to the Next Level
Level 0: Oblivious	Unaware of the need for professionally produced publications. Publications are produced by anyone who is available and has time.	None	Staffing with professional technical communicators
Level 1: Ad hoc	Technical communicators act independently to produce publications with little or no coordination. They may be assigned to different technical managers.	None	Development of a style guide
Level 2: Rudimentary	The beginning pieces of a process are going into place. Some coordination occurs among the technical communicators to assure consistency, but enforcement is not strong.	None to very little	Introduction of some project planning

---

1. Table and description from JoAnn T. Hackos, *Managing Your Documentation Projects* (New York: John Wiley & Sons, 1994), p. 47–48. Used with permission.

Table B-1   Process Maturity Levels of Documentation Organizations (Continued)

Level	Description	Publications Project Management	Transition to the Next Level
Level 3: Organized and repeatable	A sound development process is in place and being refined. People are being trained in the process. Project management is in the beginning stages, with senior technical communicators learning the rudiments of estimating and tracking.	Introduction of project management	Strong implementation of project planning
Level 4: Managed and sustainable	Strong project management is in place to ensure that the publications-development process works. Estimating and tracking of projects are thorough, and controls are in place to keep projects within budgets and schedules. Innovation gains importance within the strong existing structure.	Strong commitment to project management	Beginning of the implementation of more effective processes
Level 5: Optimizing	Everyone on the teams is engaged in monitoring and controlling projects. As a result, effective self-managed teams are becoming the norm. Innovations in the development process are regularly investigated and the teams have a strong commitment to continuous process improvement.	Strong commitment to project management and institution of self-managed teams	Strong and sustainable commitment to continuous process improvement

Establishing the Value of the Department

If you want to expand your department, the first step is usually to convince management of its value. However, measuring the "value added" of accurate, comprehensive documentation written by professional technical communicators is not easy. Your focus is on added ease-of-use for the user, in the product interface as well as the documentation, but that is often not as important an argument to management as actual costs saved.

B

This section provides some ways in which you can show how good documentation adds value, and some metrics from other studies you can use.[2]

Accounting for Value Added

Traditional accounting practices often make showing the benefits of improving quality very difficult. For example, many accounting systems still track costs by department rather than project. If customer support costs go down, the customer support group looks good. The documentation group doesn't get any credit for reducing support costs, even if good documentation contributed substantially to the reduction.

Many accounting systems are still based on a manufacturing model rather than a labor-intensive service model. For example, a documentation group that is measured only on pages per day appears to cost more if their higher-quality documents have fewer pages. Value that they are adding through activities other than writing and production (such as interface evaluation) or the greater benefits of shorter documents may not be reflected in the accounting reports.

Tracking Avoided Costs and Costs Saved

Keep in mind that when considering the value added by a professional publications staff and good documentation, costs avoided are as significant as costs saved. For example, if a company gets 100,000 support calls a year at a cost of $30 a call, and if better documentation reduces the call volume by 10 percent (either the number of calls or a shorter duration of call), the technical communicators save the company $300,000 a year.

Another aspect you can point out is the cost per problem at different points in the product development cycle. Problems found in the writing/editing cycle are much less expensive to fix than problems found once the product is in the field.

Measures that show *increased benefits* resulting from good documentation include:

- More sales
- Increased productivity
- A higher percentage of forms or response cards returned
- Forms or response cards returned more quickly
- More users' problems identified early in the process

---

2. The material in this section is based on information from G. Redish, "Adding Value as a Professional Technical Communicator," *Technical Communication* 42:1 (1995), p. 26–39. Used with permission.

Measures that show *reduced costs* resulting from good documentation include:

- Fewer support calls; lower support costs
- Less need for training; lower training costs
- Fewer requests for maintenance; lower maintenance costs
- Less time needed for translation; lower translation costs
- Less effort (time, lines of code, rework) needed when technical communicators are involved early in the development process than when they are not
- Lower costs for writing, paper, printing, and so on because technical communicators showed developers that they did not need all the documentation they were planning
- Fewer errors in specifications written by technical communicators than in specifications written by engineers

When trying to find ways to illustrate *value added* by good documentation, consider the following techniques:

- Estimating avoidable costs from historical data (for example, costs of writing and sending updates and bulletins about problems and solutions, support costs, and costs to the customer's company)
- Comparing two documents or two situations where one used the services of publications personnel and the other did not (for example, a prior version of a document that has been revised, or users of the documentation vs. those who do not have access to it)

Establishing Expertise

Companies, especially those with fledgling publications groups, often regard documentation as merely writing down what the product does. You should also try to establish a role as the user advocate, so that you can offer your expertise during the project development stage in areas such as interface evaluation, menu item and error message wording, usability, and so on. If you encounter resistance to early writer involvement, point out that problems like inconsistent interface features take much less time, and therefore money, to correct at early stages in product development than if the writers are not involved until the actual writing cycle begins.

B

Funding the Publications Department

Once you've convinced management that your department should be expanded, you may be asked to help determine how your publications department is funded.

Some possibilities are:

- Funding by the division to which the publications department reports regardless of who receives the documentation services. For example, a publications department might report to and be funded by the marketing division even though it is developing documentation for the engineering group.

- Funding for department personnel from the budget of the project they are documenting. The publications manager identifies the staffing level required for a given project and the positions are funded by the project's budget.

- Funding for centralized services—such as editing, illustration, and production—by the division to which the publications department reports, with individual writers funded by the project they are documenting.

Obviously, there are advantages and disadvantages to each scenario. For example, if you are a writer reporting directly to an engineering project manager, you will probably have a closer relationship with the engineers on the project than if you are a member of a separate publications department. At the same time, your concerns as a publications-oriented team member might not be taken as seriously in an engineering group as they would if you reported to a publications manager.

Determining the Roles of the Publications Team

Once you have permission to expand your staff, consider the roles your staff members need to fill. The following sections describe the roles of various publications personnel. Smaller departments or projects might need to combine these functions.

Manager

- Supervises all personnel matters: recruiting, hiring, training, supervising, and evaluating
- Plans, schedules, and may oversee projects
- Acquires and allocates resources: monetary, personnel, equipment, outside resources
- Works with project initiation, design, and planning teams

Writing Team Leader

- Coordinates and maintains the documentation plan (see "Writing a Documentation Plan" on page 201 for more details)
- Coordinates and tracks schedules
- Assigns writing tasks to individual writers and consults with them to set priorities
- Makes sure technical/hardware problems encountered by writers are resolved
- Represents the writing team at project team meetings or other department meetings relating to the project
- Holds weekly meetings of the writing team and issues weekly status reports
- Coordinates multiple technical reviews
- Serves as the liaison with the production staff

Writer

- Determines scope and contents of assigned books with input from other writing team members, marketing, usability testing, and other relevant departments
- Writes the documentation plan if there is no writing team leader (see "Writing a Documentation Plan" on page 201 for more details)
- Gathers and verifies source data, which includes attending engineering and product design meetings
- Disseminates project information to the rest of the documentation team
- Writes the documentation according to the audience and technical content defined in the documentation plan
- Develops or works with an illustrator to create illustrations
- Incorporates editorial and technical review comments
- Arranges for validity and usability testing

B

Editor

- Directs and guides the writers to write clearly and consistently, with the user in mind at all times
- Provides editorial support at all levels: developmental editing, copy editing, and proofreading (see "Editing Checklists" in Appendix C, "Checklists and Forms")
- Ensures that grammar, syntax, and spelling are correct in all documents
- In projects with more than one writer, brings the different styles of the various writers into a consistent whole, to achieve a single voice
- Maintains the project style sheet
- Keeps all writers on a project informed of stylistic decisions, title changes, and so on
- Ensures correct use of copyright and trademark information
- Checks that all figures and tables (from chapter to chapter and book to book) are consistent in style and quality, are in the right position, and (if appropriate) are numbered correctly

Graphics Designer

- Develops the overall look and design of the documentation product
- Determines how typography, use of color, and general layout of the information are handled
- Designs graphic elements that assist a reader, such as icons and glyphs
- May produce graphics for the software interface or on-line documentation
- Helps redesign the documentation format for a company, a set of documents, or a single document
- Designs packaging and manual covers

Illustrator

- Works closely with the writer to create drawings for information products
- Participates in the project documentation team and understands the material, especially on large projects
- Works with the graphics designer on projects that require numerous illustrations

Hiring Contract vs. Permanent Staff

Once you've decided who's paying for the publications staff and what they do, you can start hiring them. One of the primary decisions in this area is whether to hire permanent staff or to use contractors. Small companies may choose to hire a documentation manager who supervises a staff of contractors; larger companies may have a mixed staff of contractors and permanent writers, or hire contractors for peak loads or short-term projects only.

Advantages of Using Contractors

- *Expertise* – Full-time contractors can offer a high level of experience and professionalism. These qualities are especially important if your publications department is young and your processes are not fully in place.

- *Flexibility* – In slow times, you do not need to maintain a full staff.

- *Seeing prospective employees in real work conditions* – More and more companies are using contractors with an option to convert them to permanent staff. This enables you to see whether the employee is productive and works well in your environment.

- *Cost* – The cost per hour of contractors is necessarily higher than permanent staff, but you save on paying for health benefits and vacation, and sometimes the office space and equipment costs, of a permanent position. Also, experienced contractors can often produce documentation quickly.

Disadvantages of Using Contractors

- *Learning curve* – Contractors are usually unfamiliar with your product, your processes, and the employees of your company, whether in your own department or in other departments from which they need to gain information.

  Not only must you allow time for the contractor to "get up to speed," but the knowledge gained also departs with the contractor rather than benefiting the company.

  Also, for editors especially, lack of familiarity with your in-house style and the lack of an established relationship with in-house writers can be difficult factors to overcome.

- *Accessibility* – If contractors are working off site, they are not available for spur-of-the-moment meetings or decision-making.

B

- *Communication* – The adage "out of sight, out of mind" is unfortunately often true when you mix permanent staff and contractors. For example, sometimes tacit agreements on style or processes are made in casual hallway conversations that the contractor misses and that the on-site personnel forget to pass on.

Considerations When Hiring Contractors

After deciding to hire a contractor, make sure that you consider the following:

- *On-site time commitment* – There should be a clear understanding of how much time the contractor is expected to be on site, for meetings or other necessary commitments.

- *Tax regulations* – Make sure that you comply with the regulations of federal, state, and local tax agencies. Some payment agreements and on-site time considerations may affect whether tax agencies will consider contractors as permanent employees.

- *Non-disclosure agreement* – You should have the contractor sign a standard agreement that protects your company's proprietary information.

- *Compatible software delivery mechanism* – Make sure that the contractor has compatible software and hardware and can deliver easily into your current system.

- *Delivery of material* – Materials must be delivered to the contractor (such as updated schedules and project style sheets) and received from the contractor (such as drafts or schedule updates). You should have an easy and efficient method of delivery.

Considerations When Hiring Permanent Staff

If your company has a personnel office, hiring procedures are probably already established. However, if your hiring is less formal, you may need to consider:

- Developing job descriptions
- Determining grade or salary levels for levels of writers, editors, or illustrators
- Evaluating the level of seniority needed for a position (for example, could you use entry-level applicants or college interns?)
- Establishing the interviewing team (for example, should developers on the project be included?)
- Conducting orientation and training

Read Me First!

Scheduling

One of the more difficult tasks facing any publications department is coming up with accurate and realistic schedules, and modifying them while the project is underway. This section provides some basic information about schedule estimates and contingencies, but it is by no means exhaustive. For a list of books that deal specifically with managing documentation projects, see the section "Project Management" in Appendix A.

Estimating Task Times

Table B-2 shows a rough formula for calculating the hours needed for documentation tasks.[3] Keep in mind that these are *estimates only* and that they may vary depending upon the nature of the documentation (for example, very technical documentation is usually more time-consuming to write and edit than overview information) and outside factors such as poor source material or limited availability of subject matter experts.

Table B-2   Productivity Formulas

Activity	Formula for Calculating Hours
Writing new text	3–5 hours per page
Revising existing text	1–3 hours per page
Editing	6–8 pages per hour
Indexing	5 pages per hour
Production preparation	5 percent of all other activities
Project management	10–15 percent of all other activities

You may want to consider setting up a system to track the amount of time your staff members spend on each project, which you can use to more accurately predict the amount of time needed for future projects.

---

3. L. Fredrickson and J. Lasecke, "Planning for Factors that Affect Project Cost" *Proceedings of the 41st International Technical Communication Conference* (Arlington, VA: Society for Technical Communication, 1994), p. 357–359.

≡ B

Developing a Project Schedule

When developing the schedule, tie your deliverables to project milestones rather than calendar dates. Estimate the time before or after a milestone at which you expect to deliver the component (for example, "The first draft of the documentation will be completed two weeks after the alpha version of the software is delivered to Product Test"). That way, you can more easily adjust your documentation schedule to match the progress of the project. Be realistic in your own assessment of actual progress in other departments, such as product development and testing.

Table B-3 shows a typical publications project schedule.

Table B-3   Sample Publications Schedule

Milestone	Date Information
Engineering specification	Date from engineering
Documentation plan	Start and end dates
Alpha software delivery	Due date
First draft	Due date
Technical review	Start and end dates
Developmental edit	Same start and end dates as technical review
Usability test of draft	Same start and end dates as technical review
Index development	Same start and end dates as technical review
User interface freeze	Date from engineering
Illustrations complete	Due date
Feature/function freeze	Date from engineering
Second draft	Due date
Copy edit	Start and end dates
Validity testing	Same start and end dates as copy edit
Final draft	Due date
Proofread	Start and end dates
Final draft to production (hard-copy and on-line versions)	Due date

Be sure to keep track of changes in delivery dates, and let other departments involved in the project know if a date is going to slip. Setting expectations up front is the best way to establish credibility (and to call attention to late deliverables on which your own deliverables depend).

Documentation Process

This section walks you through the process of planning and writing documentation and of getting it reviewed.

Writing a Documentation Plan

The documentation plan informs the rest of the product team about your doc plans for the product. It should be reviewed by representatives of all departments involved with the product. It should be kept up to date throughout the project, with major changes being announced when necessary.

The documentation plan is based on input from various departments. Table B-4 provides some ideas of the type of information you might get from other departments.

Table B-4   *Documentation Plan Input From Other Departments*

Department Name	Relevant Information
Marketing	Product definition, product name, customer profile, feature/function product requirements
Development	Feature/function schedule, user interface concerns, error message data, names of experts on subject matter
Legal	Trademarks, product names
Customer Support	Customer profile, previous product troubleshooting logs, how to obtain technical support, names of experts on subject matter
Manufacturing and Operations	Part numbers, product packaging, production schedules, shipping lead time

B

Table B-5 lists the components of a typical documentation plan. It is a sample only, and not all sections are relevant to all product types or publications departments.

Table B-5   Documentation Plan Sample Topics

Topic	Content
Product information	Product name and version, brief description of the product's intended use.
Documentation resource requirements	Personnel, equipment.
Revision information	Differences from the documentation of previous versions of the product (if any).
Documentation objectives	Overall objectives of the documentation set or of each book.
Documentation overview	Full list of documentation deliverables and the format in which they will be delivered.
Documentation descriptions	Brief description of the chapters and appendixes in each book, with the estimated page counts. (If the books in the documentation set are large, they each might require a separate documentation plan.)
Documentation schedule	Publications schedule milestones and other milestones from the project schedule that affect the documentation. Publications milestones might include draft delivery dates, technical review dates, and the final document delivery date to production.
Technical review	List of technical reviewers and the projected review schedule.
Test plan	Plans for validity testing, usability testing, and, if relevant, media testing plans and dates.
Edit plan	Editing schedule and book priorities.
Localization plan	Languages into which the document will be translated, required resources, and schedule.
Documentation design	Format of the documentation components, including book sizes, on-line media, and so on.

Table B-5   Documentation Plan Sample Topics (Continued)

Topic	Content
Production plan	Printing and packaging specifications.
Issues	Any projected issues that might affect documentation, such as suspected schedule slips, engineering uncertainties, or known project design difficulties.
Critical dependencies	Items needed from other groups, including the due date and the impact if the information is not provided or is late. These might include: • Prototype delivered • Subject matter experts designated • Technical product specification received • User interface freeze • Feature/function freeze • Alpha version of working software • Installation specifications • Beta software released to testing • Technical review sign-off meeting complete • Development freeze • Final list of error messages, causes, and remedies • Confirmed product name

Coordinating With Product Development

Documentation concerns especially affect product development at two points in the schedule: during technical review and at the end of the project.

- *Technical review* – You *must* have dedicated time from your subject matter experts for them to complete a thorough and expert review of your documentation. Unfortunately, technical reviews usually occur when development is busy with last-minute engineering and bugs fixes. Management support is often crucial in making sure that the development staff take the time to review the documentation thoroughly. Documentation must be considered an important part of the product by all departments for technical review to be treated with the attention it requires.

- *Code freeze* – The other development concern is at the end of the product cycle, when you need to freeze your screen illustrations and descriptions of the product, and development is still busily fixing bugs. Make sure that the developers, and management, realize that the documentation requires production and printing lead time. They also need to realize that changes to the product after the documentation has gone to production are difficult, if not impossible, to incorporate and will cost more.

B

Writing Process

This section deals with the writing of the documentation and with the handoffs the writer must deliver.

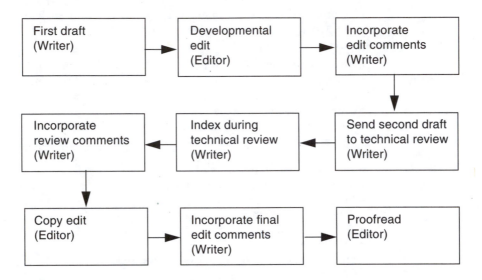

First Draft

The first draft focuses on where information goes and how it should be presented. In the writing of the first draft, the writer should focus on these tasks:

- Determine organization. Fill out outlines from the documentation plan (making adjustments where necessary) and work with other writers and the editor to define the interrelationships among the manuals.

- Ascertain where technical information is missing or incomplete and alert engineers and the other writers.

- Develop thematically unified examples (a scenario), if needed.

- Identify terminology issues and raise them for discussion and resolution.

- Develop an approach to the audience defined in the documentation plan and develop the voice appropriate for that audience.

- Develop ideas for art and screen illustrations and compile a preliminary list of figures.

Second Draft

The second draft should be as complete as the state of the software and the specifications permit. It should be fully illustrated. The writing should be polished.

In the writing of the second draft, the writer should focus on these tasks:

- Incorporate edits and comments from reviewers of the first draft.
- Revise for clarity and consistency of voice and terminology.
- Fill in the technical gaps from the first draft as information becomes available.
- Make sure that all terminology and usage decisions made since the first draft are reflected.
- Compile a list of index entries and begin to develop main entries, subentries, and cross-references.
- Arrange for a validity test (or perform each procedure yourself) for all chapters to ensure technical accuracy and completeness.
- Complete assembly of screen illustrations and incorporate other types of illustrations.

Editing Process

An ideal editorial cycle includes:

- *Developmental edit* – A review of structure and organization at the first-draft stage
- *Copy edit* – A review of readability and style at the second-draft stage
- *Proofreading* – A final review prior to production

See Appendix C for checklists describing what is covered in developmental, copy, and proofreading edits.

As your company's publications needs become greater and your publications staff begins dealing with more projects, you will probably want to develop a company style guide covering editorial and writing guidelines specific to your publications style and your product line. Besides using *Read Me First!* as a model, you may want to examine some of the books mentioned in Appendix A.

For more information on working with an editor, see Chapter 2, "Working With an Editor."

B

Illustration and Graphics Design

If your illustration and design needs are minimal, someone on your team such as a writer or publications manager may be able to handle graphics design and illustration coordination. However, as your needs increase, you should consider adding a production coordinator to your staff. This person can coordinate with outside vendors, contract for illustration and graphics design help, or hire permanent staff in this area when necessary.

Illustration Concerns

Processes for dealing with illustrations vary depending upon the type of illustrations, the availability of compatible screen capture software, whether you have in-house staff or are using contractors, and your budget.

If screen capture software is available for the operating system you are running, the writer is usually responsible for capturing the screen illustrations. The writer is the one most familiar with what the screen should illustrate and with the software being documented, and so can more efficiently set up the screen appropriately. However, you may want to send these illustrations on to an illustrator to be "cleaned up" for the best final reproduction quality.

Concept illustrations, on the other hand, usually benefit from having an illustrator render them. Not all writers are gifted artistically, and the time spent producing art is time *not* spent writing. Illustrators are also more familiar with the "language" of illustrations and can usually produce a more professional concept illustration.

The writer, illustrator, and editor should meet periodically to discuss rough sketches and specifications for illustrations.

A preliminary list of illustrations required for the project is produced by all the writers. (For a sample illustration request form and art tracking form, see Appendix C.) The writers periodically review the illustrations for their specific books with the illustrator until both are satisfied with the final art.

Note – If your documentation consists in large part of updating existing documentation for a standard set of products, consider archiving generic illustrations of your product or its basic concepts for use in future documentation.

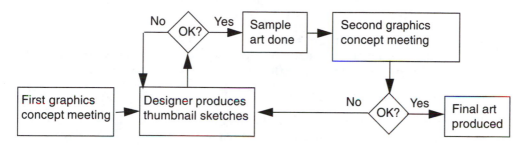

Graphics Design Process

The graphics design for your documentation set may already be established or may be standard for each book or on-line component. However, you may need a graphics design plan if you are adding new types of components to your documentation set, or if you have a new product line for which you want a different look.

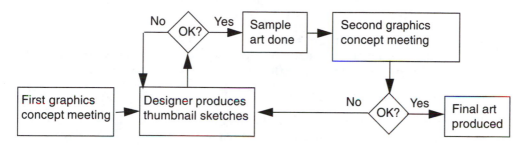

- *First graphics concept meeting* – The writers, editor, and graphics designer should hold an initial meeting to identify and discuss product concepts that could best be conveyed through graphics, page layout, and other documentation design issues. The result of this meeting is a graphics design direction for the project. A graphics designer can often also help in designing on-line tutorials or other on-line documentation.

- *Second graphics concept meeting* – A second graphics concept meeting is held to approve the final graphics design. If rework is necessary, the graphics designer either produces another sample for another review or executes the art with the final changes incorporated.

Technical Review

This section explains some of the issues related to the publications team and the reviewers during a technical review process. Remember, thorough technical review is an important contribution to the accuracy and usefulness of your documentation. Unfortunately, this is sometimes a difficult concept to convey to other groups. This section provides information on how to promote and conduct a technical review.

Make sure that you provide details about the technical review, including its schedule, in your documentation plan or during planning meetings. Emphasize the importance of having accurate documentation that is thoroughly reviewed and tested. Point out the advantages this provides to the whole company in saved support costs, a good reputation, and favorable industry reviews.

B

Make sure that the relevant departments allow time for their personnel to review the documentation, and that they know the seriousness of the review. For successful completion of a documentation project, the reviewers must be available to conduct reviews and to attend review meetings at the time specified in the documentation plan or the review cover letter. (See the sample review cover letter in Appendix C.)

Once reviewer comments have been returned and evaluated, hold a review meeting to ensure the accuracy of the documentation, resolve conflicts between reviewers, and collect final comments.

At the conclusion of the technical review and the review meeting, designated reviewers from each department should "sign off" that the documentation, with the agreed-upon changes, meets with their department's approval.

Comment Acceptance

Comments regarding technical *errors* in the documentation should be incorporated. Comments regarding technical *completeness* should be accepted or rejected depending upon the scope and intent of the documentation as specified in the documentation plan or as interpreted by the writer, writing team leader, or manager.

Comments regarding the *purpose and scope* of the manual, including the intended audience, should be accepted or rejected based upon the related material in the documentation plan.

Comments on *editorial style, organization,* or *cosmetic changes* should be accepted or rejected based upon style and design guidelines.

Participants in the Technical Review

Participants in the technical review process should ideally already be members of the project team. However, even those outside the project team (such as customer support personnel and testers) may be able to provide valuable feedback.

Departments you may want to have represented, and their review responsibilities, are listed here. You may want to provide this information (modified for your own situation) as part of the documentation plan.

Product Development

- The documentation accurately describes the technical aspects of the product.
- The text, examples, and illustrations are technically correct.
- All technical information specified in the documentation plan is included.

Product Test

- The documentation accurately describes the technical aspects of the product.
- The text, examples, and illustrations are technically correct.
- All technical information specified in the documentation plan is included.
- The procedures in all written and on-line documentation have been performed to ensure technical accuracy and completeness.

Marketing

- The documentation describes the product as it is specified in any marketing requirements document.
- The documentation is appropriate for the target audience.
- Proprietary information or information deemed inappropriate for publication outside the company is not included in the documentation.

Customer Support

- The documentation accurately describes the technical aspects of the product.
- The procedures in all written and on-line documentation have been performed to ensure technical accuracy and completeness.
- The documentation is appropriate for the target audience.
- The documentation includes information about how to obtain technical support.

Usability Testing

- The documentation is appropriate for the target audience.
- The documentation facilitates users' successful completion of tasks that the product supports.
- The instructional objectives of any tutorial material are met.

Publications Department

- The documentation conforms to current department and corporate standards and guidelines.
- The documentation is written in accordance with the documentation plan.
- The documentation is easy to read, well organized, and easy to use.
- The documentation is composed correctly: Tables and figures are clear and easy to read, there are no typographical errors, misspellings, and so on.

Legal

- The documentation properly uses all trademark and copyright conventions.
- All product names in the documentation are accurate and used correctly.

Review Meeting

The review meeting is chaired by the documentation manager or a designated representative. The sign-off reviewers designated in the documentation plan should attend the review meeting. Sign-off reviewers attending the review meeting are responsible for consolidating comments from their area into one copy and for resolving conflicting comments from different reviewers in their area prior to submission.

The writer or writing team leader should prepare an agenda of comment items. In an ideal situation where comments have been collected on line, you can distribute reports before the meeting that list those comments that have been accepted without discussion, those comments that have been rejected, and those comments that are unresolved. Otherwise, mark on the review copies those comments that are unresolved or rejected.

The agenda for the meeting should include rejected comments that reviewers still want to have considered, and unresolved comments.

The chairperson leads a discussion of each item on the agenda. Once the items have been resolved, the sign-off sheet should be distributed for representative signatures.

Often engineers and others feel that their comments regarding organization or writing style should receive as much weight as their comments on technical matters. Keep in mind, and make sure that they keep in mind, that *you* are the expert on publications, just as *they* are the experts on coding or testing.

Internationalization and Localization

If your company does a portion of its business internationally, you may need to localize or internationalize your documentation. *Internationalization* involves creating a "generic" document that can be easily translated into or used in many languages or cultures, converting any language or culture-specific references into generic ones. *Localization* involves converting a document that is specific to a language or culture into one that is specific to a different language or culture. See Chapter 4, "Writing for an International Audience," for more specific details.

Some companies simply translate their documentation into specific languages; others fully internationalize or localize the product and documentation. Although larger companies generally have a dedicated department to handle this process, others depend on the publications department.

This is a large and complicated area that requires some expertise. Decisions about the process that affect publications include:

- How soon the localized versions need to be ready after the native-language product is finished (often determined by marketing and sales concerns rather than publications resources)

- How changes to the documentation within the product release and in subsequent releases are tracked and passed on to the translators

- How long the translation cycle takes (including review and revisions)

- The document exchange formats, both hardware and software, and the method of delivery

For smaller documents, you may want to have all languages in one document; for larger documents you probably will want separate documents for each language. This decision must also take into account your company's manufacturing, product kitting, and inventory methods, and the number of copies to be printed for each locale.

On-line Documentation Considerations

Producing documentation for on-line presentation involves different concerns than printed paper documentation. This section briefly discusses some issues you need to take into account, but it is by no means comprehensive. See Appendix A for books that deal with this subject in depth.

Many companies are turning to on-line presentation of their documentation so that customers have easier access to their documentation, to save on printing and production costs, and to provide searchable linked information. If your company is considering such a move, be sure to research presentation and usability issues thoroughly.

Many issues arise when moving from print to on-line documentation. They involve writing, content, and management concerns.

B

Writing Issues

Because printed text has existed for hundreds of years, writers and readers instinctively know how to use it. On-line text, however, is new and constantly changing. People writing and using on-line text don't have the combined knowledge that comes from generations of experimentation and example. Guidelines for on-line documents are often incomplete, contradictory, or outdated.

- *Writing style* – To design on-line information, writers must change from the familiar writing style used for printed text to an unfamiliar, sometimes undefined style used for on-line presentation. Writers also often have a hard time going back and forth between the two writing styles.

- *Scheduling* – Time must be built into the schedule to allow writers and editors to develop their on-line writing style, and to transition between the printed and on-line formats.

- *Platform-specific versions* – Although some information providers use a "write-once publish-twice" scheme that presents the same documentation on line and in print, to most effectively take advantage of the benefits of on-line publishing, text should be written specifically for that medium.

Content Issues

- *Access* – You need to determine how the user will find and retrieve information, and what navigation aids you will provide.

- *Text format* – First, you must decide whether to duplicate information in both formats, or whether you will provide some information only on line and some only in print. If you choose the latter strategy, you need to decide the appropriate format for each type of information.

  One typical strategy is to provide task or brief explanatory information on line, and more in-depth or background information in print.

- *Graphics* – If you decide to provide graphics in your on-line documentation, you must decide what format they will be in, how they will be included, and whether they will be linked.

- *Hyperlinks* – Some decisions to be made about hyperlinks include which information should be linked, and whether links should be accessed only through text or also through graphics. You may also decide to limit the number of links you want in a given body of information.

- *Page design* – Type size, page size, and page layout work differently on line than in print. You must decide whether to optimize your design for on-line or print presentation, or to use two separate designs.

Read Me First!

Management Issues

- *Scheduling* – Designing and planning on-line documentation is usually more time-consuming than print presentation due to the possibility of linked information and to the ramifications of on-line display.

- *Authoring tools* – On-line documentation usually requires a different set of authoring tools than your standard word processing or desktop publishing software. These tools sometimes involve separate products for authoring and for on-line viewing.

- *Outside resources* – Support from other departments is usually required to a greater extent for on-line documentation than for print documentation. For example, you need to work more closely with graphics designers, product test, and the software integration team. When planning your on-line documentation strategy, make sure that the various organizations have agreed to provide these resources.

- *Delivery mechanism* – Will your on-line documentation be part of the interface (as is usually the case with on-line help, for example) or the product code? Your deadlines and testing procedures will be affected by this decision.

- *Integration* – How will your documentation be connected to the product? You need to find out how the user will access the on-line information, and how it will be installed and set up.

- *Testing* – Testing on-line documentation involves both the content of the documentation and the delivery media. Hyperlinks that the user can click to go rapidly to cross-referenced information, for example, are one of the benefits of many on-line delivery products. Each hyperlink must be tested to make sure that it goes to the appropriate location. If the documentation is being delivered as part of the product, it must work correctly with the product code. Finally, the medium itself must be tested to make sure that it works on all supported platforms.

- *Legal* – Presenting information on line usually means a change in how copyright and trademark issues are handled. Consult with counsel.

- *Production* – If your on-line documentation will be produced on CD-ROM media, you must determine whether it will be included with the product software or on a separate disc. This can also affect your packaging.

- *ASCII text* – Often, last-minute product changes or additions are documented in a brief on-line file in ASCII text. Consider drafting some formats for this type of presentation.

B

Final Print Production

Activities associated with the final production of hard-copy documentation are:

- Printing
- Binding
- Packaging

In larger companies, typically a separate production department handles these activities and the publications organization simply hands off the final camera-ready copy or electronic files. In smaller organizations, the publications department is responsible for these activities.

This section provides only general information about printing and production processes. See Appendix A for sources of more thorough information on these subjects.

Deciding on a Strategy

There are several factors that influence the type of printing and packaging used for documentation. Some of these include:

- *Audience* – Is the documentation aimed at in-house engineers or commercial end users? This might determine your page layout or presentation. Under what conditions will your audience use the product? This might determine whether your books need to lie flat, or whether you need to use a sturdier page weight or binding method.
- *Competitors* – How are similar products printed or packaged?
- *Distribution method* – If you sell directly to your customers, packaging can be minimal (an envelope or corrugated box), whereas if you're selling to resellers, you probably want a more professional presentation.
- *Cost* – Your operations or marketing departments will probably set a profit level for the product that includes the documentation production cost limit.

Printing Methods

While there are various ways that documents can be reproduced, the two main printing methods are offset printing and photocopying. If you need fewer than 1000 copies of your manuals, you probably want to use photocopying. For 1000 to 4000 copies, regular sheet-fed offset is usually appropriate. For over 4500 copies, you will probably need to use a printer with a web press (one that uses rolls of paper rather than sheets).

Offset Printing

Offset printing provides higher quality and may be your only choice if you are using color in illustrations or text, or photographs. Note that if you are producing camera-ready copy on a 300-dots per inch (dpi) laser printer, offset printing will not increase the quality of the output.

Offset printing requires a larger print quantity to be cost-effective. Ordering a larger quantity just to take advantage of the price break is usually not a good strategy, though, because you may be left with many copies of outdated manuals. Costs for offset printing are also influenced by other factors, including the use of color, the size of the page (influencing how much trimming is needed), and the type of paper and ink used.

Photocopying

Photocopying produces lowe-quality output, but it is more cost-effective for smaller quantities. Other costs for photocopying might include special handling if you're using an odd size of paper or special paper. Many photocopying machines today can provide rudimentary binding as well as photocopying.

Binding Methods

There are several types of binding generally available. The most common are:

- Three-ring binders
- Wire-o
- Perfect
- Saddle-stitch

Factors that influence which binding method you choose might include:

- Page size and number of pages
- Whether update insertions will be necessary
- Frequency of users' access and the environment where the book will be used
- Cost
- Customer preference

Three-Ring Binders

Three-ring binders hold standard 8.5- x 11-inch pages or other industry-standard page sizes. (For a price, you can also arrange for custom-size binders.) A big advantage to binders is that you can easily insert updates, change pages, and tabs. Covers can be slipped into plastic pockets in some binders on the front and spine, which saves binder printing costs. However, three-ring binders take up a lot of room. Users often dislike them because they are bulky and awkward to handle, and the rings can burst or rip pages.

Wire-O

Wire-o binding is much less expensive than three-ring binding, is smaller, and lies flatter. There is also much more variety available in page size. However, updates are difficult to include and the wire prevents the book title from being printed on the spine. (Wraparound covers are the workaround to this problem, but they are not very effective and add cost. Generally, users don't like them and often can't figure out how to use them.)

Perfect

Perfect binding is less expensive than either three-ring or wire-o binding, especially in large quantities. A perfect bound book usually includes the book title on its spine, making it easily identifiable on a shelf. The chief complaint about perfect-bound books in the past was that they did not lie flat, but recently developed lay-flat or flex bindings have remedied this problem. You cannot insert updates or change pages into perfect-bound books. Also, large page counts sometimes mean that pages may fall out over time.

Saddle-Stitch

Saddle-stitch binding is possible only for page counts up to 80 pages. While it is very inexpensive, you cannot insert updates or change pages into saddle-stitched books, and they are too thin to have a spine.

Packaging

The type of packaging you use should be determined in large part by how you sell your products and what your competition provides. If you sell products directly to your customers, you may not need as elaborate a packaging scheme as if you were to sell products through an external commercial vendor, where your package competes with others.

Direct-to-customer packaging could be as simple as a padded envelope or corrugated box.

The type of *commercial* packaging you choose could be influenced by several factors, including:

- What your competitors produce and, therefore, what customers expect.
- The number of different pieces delivered. For example, do you have several disks, several manuals, a quick reference card, and a warranty card? Or do you have a single disk and a single manual?
- Your budget.

If you are new to dealing with commercial packaging, you may want to go through your printer to find a reputable packaging source. You can also go through a broker, who puts together a whole production package, finding and dealing with printing and packaging vendors, for a fee.

When you find a packaging vendor, be sure to have the vendor produce prototypes of several packaging designs, and ask the pros and cons of each. You will probably have to provide the page counts for your manuals, and the number and type of other components in the package, before a realistic prototype can be produced.

Working With Outside Vendors

The best way to find a reputable printer or production broker is to ask people who are in the same geographic area and industry that you are. Ask printers or brokers about their experience with your type of product, or other jobs they have done for people in similar industries.

If your printing and packaging needs are relatively simple, you can probably use a printer who has less experience with your particular product area. However, you will be expected to provide the printer with camera-ready copy and all the information needed for the job.

If your needs are more complex or you have little experience in this area, you will probably need to spend more time finding a vendor who is right for you. Experienced printers can provide you with professional advice and samples, and the pros and cons of various printing methods, paper, ink, and so on. But you have to ask! Larger printers often have account representatives for larger customers who can offer suggestions and get answers for you.

If you suspect your printing or packaging needs are very complex, or you do not have either the expertise or the staff to investigate vendors, you may want to find a broker. Brokers quote a fee for your whole job, and take on the responsibility of finding and dealing with vendors, procuring packaging samples, and so on.

B

Post-Production Considerations

After the documentation is delivered to production, your work is not done. You should have a plan in place to deal with last-minute product changes or inaccuracies in the documentation. Also, if the product documentation is likely to be revised, you should collect and maintain information that will help with the next version.

Handling Post-Production Revisions

Despite your best efforts, you may discover technical inaccuracies after the documentation is produced, either from omissions or from changes to the product. Therefore, allocations of monetary and staff resources to the project must continue even after the date the final documentation is delivered to production.

Typical ways to correct documentation inaccuracies include:

- *On-line files on the product disks* – These can cover documentation inaccuracies and last-minute product revisions.

- *Replacement pages* – Errors in limited locations in printed manuals can be corrected through replacement pages that are inserted individually by users. These generally ship with the product and are accompanied by a card or insert listing all replacement pages.

- *Documentation update package* – A last-minute change to the product that has ramifications throughout the documentation may require too many change pages to make replacement pages feasible. In this case, you may want to include a documentation update package, which explains the exact changes that need to be made to specific pages, including the paragraph and line location and the information to be added or deleted. However, this should be the solution of last resort.

Note – If your company sells directly to customers rather than through a third-party commercial distributor, you can issue change pages or update packages through your distribution channel or sales staff even after the product ships.

Make sure that customer support, marketing, localization, and sales personnel know about the inaccuracies and the steps taken to correct them.

Maintaining Project Continuity

Once a product has shipped, your first impulse may be to try to forget about it as soon as possible. This will only make your job more difficult when you have to revise the documentation for the next version. Some of the information you may want to save or document about a project includes:

- The location of on-line documentation files. Delete irrelevant files such as earlier versions of text or graphics. You may want to establish a central archive where final files are kept.

- While the details are still fresh in your mind, conduct a *post-mortem meeting* with the documentation team and write down a brief project review. Document anything that might be helpful, for example:

  - Processes that didn't work as anticipated or could be modified to work better

  - Controversies that arose (even if they were resolved, having a record of each controversy could prove useful later)

  - Issues that affected the schedule that might recur during the next cycle

  - Subject matter experts or other helpful project team members who were not official reviewers or project team members

- Technical review comments from all official reviewers.

- Edits or review comments that you didn't have time to incorporate for this version, but that should appear in a future version.

- Product information that you didn't have time to incorporate for this version, but that should appear in a future version.

B

Read Me First!

Checklists and Forms

This appendix provides samples of common publications forms and checklists. You may need to modify them to reflect your own company processes.

The checklists in this appendix are:

- Manuscript tracking chart
- Request for editing
- Editing checklists
- Editorial style sheet
- Artwork request form
- Technical review cover letter
- Authorization to produce document
- Print specification

Manuscript Tracking Chart

Document title: _____

Project: _____

Writer: _____ No. of pages: _____

Edit Requested	Sent to Editor (1st review)	Returned to Writer (1st review)	Sent to Editor (2nd review)	Returned to Writer (2nd review)	Notes
Alpha					
Develop. edit					
Copy edit					
Proofread					
Release check					
Beta					
Develop. edit					
Copy edit					
Proofread					
Release check					
FCS					
Develop. edit					
Copy edit					
Proofread					
Release check					

Checked: ❏ Front matter   ❏ Back matter   ❏ Cross-references   ❏ Spelling

Dates of files to production:

   Alpha _____   Beta _____   FCS_____   Print _____

Request for Editing

Document title: _____   Product code name: _____

Writer: _____

Phone no.: _____   Email address: _____

Number of pages: _____   Date submitted: _____   Return by: _____

Target audience: _____

Type of edit requested: ❑ Developmental   ❑ Copy   ❑ Proofread

Development stage: ❑ Alpha   ❑ Beta   ❑ FCS
                   ❑ Other: _____

Is this document part of a set?   ❑ yes   ❑ no

      Name of set: _____

Has this document been edited before? ❑ yes   ❑ no

   Editor: _____   Date of prior edit: _____

   Type of edit: _____

   Were comments incorporated into this draft? ❑ yes   ❑ no

Do specific sections need particular attention?   ❑ yes   ❑ no

   If so, which ones? _____

Does the set have a style sheet?   ❑ yes   ❑ no

   If so, is it included for the editor? ❑ yes   ❑ no

Check for the following items before giving a book to the editor:

❑   Title page, credits page, TOC, LOF, LOT, and preface are current.
❑   Glossary and index are complete and current.
❑   Page numbers and footers are correct.
❑   There are no unexplained blank pages.
❑   Graphics are incorporated or content and placement are indicated.
❑   Cross-references are updated.
❑   Trademarked terms are marked appropriately on first reference in text.
❑   Spelling checker was run on all files.

Comments? _____

_____

_____

C

Editing Checklists

This section contains checklists for a developmental edit, copy edit, and proofreading.

Developmental Editing Checklist

Structure and Organization

- ❏ Audience definition, purpose of document, and how to use the book are clear.
- ❏ Information is appropriately presented for the audience.
- ❏ Concepts flow logically.
- ❏ Superfluous or redundant material is eliminated.
- ❏ Heads are useful, descriptive, and specific.
- ❏ Information is easy to find.
- ❏ Information is task-oriented where appropriate.
- ❏ Reference and conceptual information are eliminated from task descriptions.
- ❏ Distinctions between parts and chapters are clear.

Writing

- ❏ Reader context is established and reinforced.
- ❏ Tone is appropriate for the reader and to the focus of the book.
- ❏ Critical information is covered clearly.
- ❏ Task-oriented writing is clear; user actions and system actions are distinct.
- ❏ Assumptions are clearly supported.
- ❏ Writing and layout are optimized for on-line presentation.

Style

- ❏ Terms are used consistently and appropriately.
- ❏ Terms are defined and used in context correctly.
- ❏ Terms and abbreviations avoid jargon and follow guidelines for localization.
- ❏ Documentation set conventions are established and followed.

Formatting and Layout

- ❏ Book conforms to company publications standards.
- ❏ Standard templates and formats are used.

Graphics

❑ Graphics appear where needed.
❑ Artwork is integrated within the text.
❑ Tables, figures, and illustrations are used effectively and appropriately.
❑ Illustrations follow artwork and localization guidelines.

New Elements

❑ New graphics or presentation techniques are identified and used effectively.
❑ Innovations meet company design standards.

C

Copy Editing Checklist

Readability

❏ Sentences are clear, direct, and concise.
❏ Repetition is used effectively.
❏ Parallel structure is used effectively.

Style

❏ Heads, lists, and sentences have parallel construction.
❏ Headings follow hierarchy guidelines.
❏ Voice and tone are consistent.

Transitions

❏ Text is easy to follow.
❏ Information is complete and appropriately placed.
❏ Transitions between parts, chapters, and sections are clear.
❏ Transitions are effective on screen and on paper.
❏ Cross-references are correct, worthwhile, and sufficient.

Grammar

❏ Sentences are complete.
❏ Subjects and verbs, and pronouns and antecedents agree.
❏ Verb tense is consistent.
❏ Modifiers are used appropriately.
❏ Word choice and sentence structure follow guidelines for localization.
❏ Long sentences are divided for readability and localization.

Punctuation, Capitalization, and Spelling

❏ Punctuation follows editorial and documentation set guidelines.
❏ Capitalization is consistent and follows editorial and documentation set guidelines.
❏ Spelling is consistent and follows editorial and documentation set guidelines.

Read Me First!

Mechanics

- ❏ Typeface conventions are followed in all book elements.
- ❏ Product names are used correctly and consistently.
- ❏ Trademarks are used correctly.
- ❏ New terms are defined and appear in a glossary, if there is one.
- ❏ Abbreviations and acronyms follow editorial and localization guidelines.
- ❏ Numbers and symbols follow editorial and localization guidelines.
- ❏ Cross-references are punctuated correctly and refer to the intended target.
- ❏ Numbered lists and steps are used appropriately and are numbered correctly.
- ❏ Figures and tables are referred to in preceding text.
- ❏ Table continuations are noted correctly.
- ❏ Notes, Cautions, and Warnings are used correctly.
- ❏ Jump tables are used correctly.
- ❏ Footnotes are used correctly.
- ❏ Running footers and page numbers are correct.

Formatting and Layout

- ❏ Book conforms to company publications standards.
- ❏ Standard templates and formats are used.
- ❏ Page breaks and line breaks are effective.

Graphics

- ❏ Graphics are consistent throughout the book.
- ❏ Illustrations follow artwork and localization guidelines.
- ❏ Figure callouts are capitalized correctly and are in the correct font.

☰ C

Front Matter

❏ Title page has correct title, part number, and revision number.
❏ Credits page is current and trademarks (including third-party trademarks) are listed.
❏ Table of contents includes correct heads and is formatted correctly.
❏ Figures and tables are listed in the table of contents.
❏ The preface uses the correct template and contains correct chapter numbers, titles, and descriptions.
❏ The typographical conventions section within the preface is current.
❏ Page numbers at the bottom of the pages are correct.

Back Matter

❏ Appendixes are in the correct order.
❏ Templates and formats are used correctly in appendixes and glossaries.
❏ Bibliography is presented correctly.
❏ Glossary terms are alphabetized, appropriate for audience, and defined clearly.
❏ Index is complete, double-posted effectively, and formatted correctly.
❏ Page numbers are correct.

Proofreading Checklist

Front Matter

- ❏ Title page has correct title, part number, and revision number.
- ❏ Credits page is current and trademarks (including third-party ones) are listed.
- ❏ Table of contents includes correct heads and page number references, and is formatted correctly.
- ❏ Figures and tables are listed in the table of contents.
- ❏ The preface uses the correct template and contains correct chapter numbers, titles, and descriptions.

Back Matter

- ❏ Appendixes are in the correct order.
- ❏ Templates and formats are used correctly in appendixes and glossaries.
- ❏ Bibliography is correctly presented.
- ❏ Glossary is correctly presented.
- ❏ Index is formatted correctly and alphabetized according to company publications standards.

Grammar

- ❏ Sentences are complete.
- ❏ Subjects and verbs, and pronouns and antecedents agree.
- ❏ Verb tense is consistent.
- ❏ Modifiers are used appropriately.

Punctuation, Capitalization, and Spelling

- ❏ Punctuation follows editorial and documentation set guidelines.
- ❏ Capitalization is consistent and follows editorial and documentation set guidelines.
- ❏ Spelling is consistent and follows editorial and documentation set guidelines.

C

Mechanics

❏ Typeface conventions are followed in all book elements.

❏ Product names are used correctly and consistently.

❏ Trademarks are used correctly.

❏ New terms are defined and appear in a glossary, if there is one.

❏ Abbreviations and acronyms follow editorial and localization guidelines.

❏ Numbers and symbols follow localization guidelines.

❏ Cross-references are punctuated correctly and refer to the intended target.

❏ Numbered lists and steps are used appropriately and are numbered correctly.

❏ Figures and tables are numbered correctly.

❏ Table continuations are noted correctly.

❏ Jump table page number references are correct.

❏ Footnotes are used correctly.

❏ Page footers and numbers are correct.

❏ Change bars do not appear.

Formatting and Layout

❏ Book conforms to company publications standards.

❏ Standard templates and formats are used.

❏ Page breaks and line breaks are effective.

Graphics

❏ Figure callouts are capitalized correctly and are in the correct font.

❏ Artwork is aligned correctly on the page.

Editorial Style Sheet

Document title: _____ Project: _____

Writer: _____ Editor: _____

Date: _____

A B C	D E F	G H I

J K L	M N O	P Q R

S T U	V W X	Y Z Numbers

Cover capitalization, spelling, hyphenation

(n) noun   (v) verb   (a) adj preceding noun
(pa) predicate adjective   (col) collective noun   (s) singular
(pl) plural   (TM) trademark   (R) registered trademark

C

Abbreviations

Trademarked Terms

Special Font Conventions

Miscellaneous Notes

Read Me First!

Artwork Request Form

All requests should be accompanied by a sketch, existing art, or a photo for each illustration. Mark all accompanying material with its corresponding control number or with "For Reference Only."

For *new* drawings, include a sketch, a marked-up copy of other art, or a photo.

For *existing* or *revision* drawings, include the control number, figure caption, or a marked-up copy of the drawing.

Full manual title: _____

Full manual part number: _____

Requestor: _____ Phone no.: _____

Date due to writer (art delivered for proofing by midnight): _____

Document is: ❏ Beta ❏ FCS ❏ Other

Document created in: ❏ Frame ❏ Other

No.	Figure caption to be used in this manual (and used in previous manuals, if different)	Existing Control No.	**Column for Illustrator Use Only** New /Rev. Control No.
1			

C

Technical Review Cover Letter

TO: *Reviewer List*
FROM: *Writer Name*
SUBJECT: Technical Review of *Name of Book*
DATE: *Date*

The attached manuscript is the technical review version of *Name of Book*. Please review the entire manuscript, paying special attention to the notes/questions to reviewers. All open issues and unanswered questions must be resolved for this technical review to be complete.

I would appreciate your general comments as well as specific answers to the issues raised in the notes. Please give detailed and thorough responses. Also, please address the specific review responsibilities of your department.

[*Add any comments regarding specific issues/content.*]

Your review must be returned by 5 p.m. on *Date*. After reviewing your responses, I will discuss any discrepancies at the technical review sign-off meeting, which will be held:

> *Date*, at *Time*
> *Name* Conference Room

Due to the tight production schedule, please make wording or style suggestions only if they affect the technical accuracy of the text.

Thank you very much for your attention to this document. Your comments are appreciated and contribute greatly to improving the quality of *Company Name* documentation.

Authorization to Produce Document

Book Title: _____

Book Part Number: _____

Writer: _____

Path: _____

❑ One clean copy of document given to Production Coordinator

❑ Authorizations signed off

❑ Permissions set for directory and above

❑ Directory cleared of backup and other extraneous files

Approvals

Editor: _____ Date: _____

Proofreader: _____ Date: _____

Writing Manager: _____ Date: _____

Comments

_____

_____

_____

_____

For Production Use Only

Transfer location: _____

PostScript files location: _____

Archive location: _____

Database: _____

PostScript files transmitted to: _____

≡ C

Print Specification

Date:

Contact name
Contact phone no.

Company name
Company address
Company address
Fax number

Printing specification for: _____

Product description: _____

Documents to vendor (date): _____

Product ship date: _____

Quantity to print: _____

Manuals: (If the documentation set is small, fill in the table below. For larger jobs, attach a list of manuals, page counts, and the preferred binding method.)

Part Number	Title	Page Count	Binding

Format size: _____

Text stock: _____

Cover stock: _____

Cover art: _____

Tabs: _____

Cards: _____

Labels: _____

Special boxes or cartons: _____

Media: _____

Printing process: _____

Proofing requirements: _____

_____

Assembly instructions: _____

_____

General comments: _____

_____

_____

Please provide _____ with __ ___check copies at time of first customer ship.

Return all original hand-off material to _____ at completion of job.

C

Index

documentation process (*continued*)
  reviewing, 203, 207–210, 234
  writing process, 204–205
dogleg leader lines, 41
double quotes ("), *See* quotation marks
    (","")
double-dagger (‡), for table footnotes,
    125
double-posting, in indexes, 161, 161–162,
    164, 172
drafts, 204–205

E

editing, 10–14
  checklists for, 224–230
  copy
    checklist for, 226–228
    described, 11, 205
    style sheets for, 13, 52, 231–232
    timing of, 11, 12
  cycle of, 205
  developmental
    checklist for, 224–225
    described, 11, 205
    timing of, 10, 12
  for house style, 11
  indexes, 170–178
  marks for, 13–14
  mechanical, 11
  planning ahead for, 12
  proofreading
    checklist for, 229–230
    described, 11, 205
    marks for, 13–14
    timing of, 10, 11, 12
  Request for Editing form, 12, 223
  standards for, 181
  style guides for, 183–184, 205
  submitting documents for, 12
  time required for, 199
  timing of, 10–11, 12
  types of, 10–11, 205

Editorial Style Sheet form, 231–232
editors, role of, 9–10, 12, 196
electronic communication
  citing in bibliographies, 133
  proprietary information in, 65, 66
ellipsis marks (…)
  in menus, 141
  when to use, 79
em dash (—), 78
email messages
  citing in bibliographies, 133
  proprietary information in, 65, 66
emphasis
  Cautions and Warnings, 133–135
  in indexes, 158
  italics for, 69
  quotation marks for, 93
  for text, 146
employee personnel information
    See also publications departments,
        staffing
  proprietary information in, 65
en dash (–)
  in lists, 120
  when to use, 78
encapsulated PostScript (EPS), 20
endnotes, 131
error messages, 93, 128
estimating task times, *See* time require-
    ments
exclamation point (!), with quotation
    marks, 94
expertise, establishing for publications
    department, 193

F

figures
    See also callouts
  capitalizing word "figure", 68, 129
  captions for, capitalizing, 69
  checklists for, 225, 227, 230

Internal Use Only proprietary label, 65, 66
international audiences, 47–55
  See also internationalization;
    localization
  aesthetics, 51
  color usage, 51
  contact information, 48
  copyrights, 60
  cultural and geographic sensitivity, 48, 55
  date format, 48
  defining and using terms, 52
  grammar and word usage, 53–54
  graphics, 49–51
  holiday references, 48
  humor, 48
  idioms and adages, 48
  illustrations, 49–51
  irony, 48
  jargon, 52
  location examples, 48
  numbers, 54–55
  recommended reading, 184
  screen examples, 49–51
  sentence length, 53
  symbols, 54–55
  time format, 48
  units of measurement, 54
international terms
  symbols replacing, 133
  typographic conventions for, 146
internationalization
  See also international audiences
  defined, 47, 210
  overview, 210–211
  recommended reading, 184
introductory constructs, commas and, 77
isometric drawings, 20
italics
  for emphasis, 69
  index cross-references and, 152

for initial definition of terms, 52
for titles, 129
as typographic convention, 129, 144, 145, 146

J
jargon
  avoiding, 3
  international audiences and, 52
jokes, *See* humor
jump tables, 127

K
key combinations
  capitalizing, 69
  hyphenating, 81
keys
  capitalizing name of, 68
  typographic conventions for, 144, 147
  writing about, 142

L
labels
  product, copyrighting, 58
  proprietary, 65–66
law issues, *See* legal department; legal guidelines
lay-flat bindings, 216
layouts, *See* formatting
leader lines, 35–46
  aligning with callouts, 38
  angles of, 39
  crossed, 45
  crossing drawing lines, 46
  dogleg, 41
  length of, 37
  radiated, 44
  spacing from callout, 37
  taboos, 45
  when not to use, 36
leaders, *See* leader lines

legal department
   See also legal guidelines
   documentation plan and, 201
   technical review and, 210
   working with, 57, 62, 65
legal guidelines, 57–66
   contractors, 60, 198
   copyrights, 57–60
   non-disclosure agreements, 198
   proprietary information, 57,
      64–66, 198
   recommended reading, 184
   trade secrets, 57, 60
   trademarks, 57, 61–64
   working with legal department, 57,
      62, 65
length of sentences, international
      audiences and, 53
letters, single, quotation marks
      around, 93
line drawings, 21
line editing, *See* copy editing
lists, 118–121
   See also checklists
   alignment, 118
   capitalizing entries, 119
   described, 118
   grammatical rules for, 118, 119
   introducing, 119
   numbered, 118, 121
   punctuating, 119–120
   steps vs., 118
   types of, 118
   unnumbered (bulleted), 118, 120
      boldface used in, 121
      capitalization and, 68
      en dashes in, 79
      when to use, 118, 120

localization
   See also international audiences
   defined, 47, 210
   overview, 210–211
   recommended reading, 184
lowercase letters, plural of, 74

M

man pages, typographic conventions
      for, 147
managers
   See also project management
   role of, 194
manufacturing department, documenta-
      tion plan and, 201
Manuscript Tracking Chart form, 222
marketing department
   documentation plan and, 201
   print production process and, 214
   technical review and, 209
maturity levels, of publications
      departments, 190–191
measurements, *See* units of measurement
mechanics
   defined, 67
   editing checklists for, 227, 230
menus in windows, 140
   typographic conventions for, 147
messages, error, 128
metric system
   See also units of measurement
   international audiences and, 54
   U.S. audiences and, 99
minus sign (-), 78
modifiers, compound
   capitalizing, 69
   hyphenating, 72, 80
mouse terminology, 137
multivolume sets
   global index for, 177–178
   style sheets and, 13

N

names
    See also file names; titles
    style sheets and, 13
Need-to-Know proprietary label, 65, 66
negative numbers, 78
    See also numbers and numerals
non-disclosure agreements, 198
Notes, 133–134
    See also endnotes; footnotes
    indexing, 155, 160
notes and legends, in illustrations, 26
nouns
    common (generic)
        capitalization and, 68
        trademarks and, 62, 63
    possessive of, 73
    proper, capitalization and, 67
numbered lists, 118, 121
    See also lists
    capitalizing, 119
    introducing, 119
    punctuating, 119
    when to use, 118
numbered steps, *See* steps (instructions)
numbering systems
    for figures, 18
    for part dividers, 136
    for section heads, 118
    for table captions, 124
numbers and numerals, 70–72
    abbreviated, 73
    en dashes and, 78
    fractions, 72, 81
    international audiences and, 54–55
    negative, 78
    plurals of, 74
    punctuating, 72
    spelling out, 71, 72
    style sheets and, 13
    when to use, 71

O

object code
    See also software
    copyrighting, 58
    proprietary information in, 64
object-oriented images, 20
offset printing, 215
on-line documents
    content issues, 212
    copyrighting, 58
    management issues, 213
    producing, 211–213
    recommended reading, 185
    writing issues and, 212
on-screen buttons, typographic
        conventions for, 147
operations department
    documentation plan and, 201
    print production process and, 214
outside contractors, *See* contractors
outside vendors, print production
        process and, 217

P

packaging, 214, 216
page breaks, in indexes, 176–177
page design, on-line vs. printed
        documentation, 213
    See also design
page ranges
    dashes in, 78
    indexes and, 150, 152, 174, 178
parentheses ()
    brackets and, 74
    cautions about using, 91
    placement of, 92
    when to use, 91–92
part dividers, 136
participles
    lists and, 121
    steps and, 122

"See also" cross-references, *See* cross-references

"See" cross-references, *See* cross-references

semicolon (;)
    independent clauses and, 76
    in indexes, 153
    quotation marks and, 93
    when to use, 94

sentence structure
    international audiences and, 53
    for lists, 118–121
    for steps, 122–123
    verbatim commands and, 92

sentence-style callouts, 25

sequential callouts, 34

series
    commas and, 76
    semicolons and, 94

service marks, 61

sets of books
    See also global index
    style sheets and, 13

sexist language, avoiding, 4–6

SGML (standard generalized markup language), recommended reading, 187

single letters, quotation marks around, 93

single quote ('), international audiences and, 54

singular form, in indexes, 171

slang, 3, 52

slash, international audiences and, 55

software
    Cautions and, 134
    code examples, 127
    code freeze, 203
    copyrighting, 58, 60
    proprietary information in, 64
    Warnings and, 135

source code
    See also software
    copyrighting, 58, 60
    examples, 127
    proprietary information in, 64

specifications, proprietary information in, 65

spelling out
    abbreviations and acronyms, 52, 62, 64, 98
    numbers, 71, 72

spelling, verifying
    checklists for, 226, 229
    for indexes, 171
    style sheets and, 13
    for text, 11, 12

spine of books, trademarks on, 62

staffing, *See* contractors; publications departments, staffing

standard generalized markup language (SGML), recommended reading, 187

standards
    for editing, 181
    for writing, 180–181

steps
    capitalizing, 122
    described, 118, 122
    how to write, 122–123
    imperative mood for, 122, 123
    introducing, 122
    lists vs., 118
    screen captures and, 122
    single-step procedures, 122
    when to use, 122

style checklists, 224, 226

style guides
    in-house, 205
    platform, 183–184

Read Me First!

time requirements
    estimating for tasks, 154, 199
    for indexing, 154, 199
    scheduling, 199–200
    tracking productivity, 199
timing, of editing, 10–11, 12
title pages, trademarks in, 62, 64
titles
    of book, 129, 130
    capitalizing, 69
    chapter, 129, 130
        quotation marks around, 93
        trademarks in, 62, 64
    of figure, 129
    of table, 124–125
tracking
    cost savings, 192
    delivery date changes, 200
    Manuscript Tracking Chart
        form, 222
    productivity, 199
trade names, trademarks vs., 61, 62
trade secrets, 57, 60
trademarks, 57, 61–64
    abbreviations and, 62, 64, 98
    acronyms and, 62, 64, 98
    as adjectives modifying common
        nouns, 62–63
    described, 61
    first use in text, 61, 62, 64
    proper use of, 61–64
    registered, 61, 62
    symbol for, 62
    symbol placement, 62, 64
    third-party, 64
    trade names vs., 61, 62
    types of, 61
    unregistered, 61, 62
transitions, checklist for, 226
translation, *See* international audiences;
       internationalization; localization
"type," using the term, 96

typographic conventions, 143–147
    See also fonts
    assigning to text, 143
    explained in preface, 144–146
    indexes, 151, 152, 153
    when to use, 143
typography
    See also fonts
    international audiences and, 51
    recommended reading, 185

U

units of measurement
    See also metric system
    abbreviating, 99, 100–113
    fractions and, 72
    international audiences and, 54
    plurals of, 99
UNIX, typographic conventions for,
       143, 147
unnumbered (bulleted) lists, 118, 120
    capitalization and, 68, 120
    en dashes in, 79
    introducing, 119
    punctuating, 119–120
updates, *See* revisions
uppercase letters, plural of, 74
usability testing department
    See also testing
    technical review and, 209
usage of common computer terms, 95–96
user input, typographic conventions
       for, 147
user interfaces
    See also graphical user interfaces
        (GUIs)
    recommended reading, 185

≡

V

valuation, of publications departments, 191–193

variable names
    capitalizing, 69
    typographic conventions for, 147

vendors
    See also contractors
    print production process and, 217

verbs
    for graphical user interfaces (GUIs), 141
    indexes and, 158
    lists and, 121
    for mouse actions, 141
    steps and, 122, 123
    subject-verb agreement, 11

W

Warnings
    indexing, 155, 160
    using, 133, 135

web presses, 214

white papers, copyrighting, 58

widow lines, in indexes, 177

windows
    controls, 139
    elements in, 138–140
    typographic conventions for, 147
    writing about, 138, 142

wire-o binding, 216

word processor tags, copy editing
        and, 11

word usage
    See also terminology
    international audiences and, 53–54

works for hire, 60

World Wide Web (WWW)
    citing documents in bibliographies, 133
    copyrighting documents, 58
    recommended reading, 188

wraparound covers, 216

writers
    and creating illustrations, 15
    and editors, 7, 9–10
    improving writing style, 6–7
    role of, 195
    screen captures and, 206

writing
    See also editing; writing style
    checklist for, 224
    first draft, 204
    process of, 204–205
    second draft, 205
    standards for, 180–181
    style guides for, 205
    time required for, 199

writing style, 1–6
    ambivalence, 54, 80
    anticipating readers's questions, 4
    concise, 2
    consistent, 4
    humor and, 2, 48
    importance of, 1
    improvement of, 6
    jargon and, 3, 52
    sexist language and, 4–6

writing team leader, role of, 195

LICENSE AGREEMENT AND LIMITED WARRANTY

READ THE FOLLOWING TERMS AND CONDITIONS CAREFULLY BEFORE OPENING THIS DISK PACKAGE. THIS LEGAL DOCUMENT IS AN AGREEMENT BETWEEN YOU AND PRENTICE-HALL, INC. (THE "COMPANY"). BY OPENING THIS SEALED DISK PACKAGE, YOU ARE AGREEING TO BE BOUND BY THESE TERMS AND CONDITIONS. IF YOU DO NOT AGREE WITH THESE TERMS AND CONDITIONS, DO NOT OPEN THE DISK PACKAGE. PROMPTLY RETURN THE UNOPENED DISK PACKAGE AND ALL ACCOMPANYING ITEMS TO THE PLACE YOU OBTAINED THEM FOR A FULL REFUND OF ANY SUMS YOU HAVE PAID.

1.	**GRANT OF LICENSE:** In consideration of your payment of the license fee, which is part of the price you paid for this product, and your agreement to abide by the terms and conditions of this Agreement, the Company grants to you a nonexclusive right to use and display the copy of the enclosed software program (hereinafter the "SOFTWARE") on a single computer (i.e., with a single CPU) at a single location so long as you comply with the terms of this Agreement. The Company reserves all rights not expressly granted to you under this Agreement.

2.	**OWNERSHIP OF SOFTWARE:** You own only the magnetic or physical media (the enclosed disks) on which the SOFTWARE is recorded or fixed, but the Company retains all the rights, title, and ownership to the SOFTWARE recorded on the original disk copy(ies) and all subsequent copies of the SOFTWARE, regardless of the form or media on which the original or other copies may exist. This license is not a sale of the original SOFTWARE or any copy to you.

3.	**COPY RESTRICTIONS:** This SOFTWARE and the accompanying printed materials and user manual (the "Documentation") are the subject of copyright. You may not copy the Documentation or the SOFTWARE, except that you may make a single copy of the SOFTWARE for backup or archival purposes only. You may be held legally responsible for any copying or copyright infringement which is caused or encouraged by your failure to abide by the terms of this restriction.

4.	**USE RESTRICTIONS:** You may not network the SOFTWARE or otherwise use it on more than one computer or computer terminal at the same time. You may physically transfer the SOFTWARE from one computer to another provided that the SOFTWARE is used on only one computer at a time. You may not distribute copies of the SOFTWARE or Documentation to others. You may not reverse engineer, disassemble, decompile, modify, adapt, translate, or create derivative works based on the SOFTWARE or the Documentation without the prior written consent of the Company.

5.	**TRANSFER RESTRICTIONS:** The enclosed SOFTWARE is licensed only to you and may not be transferred to any one else without the prior written consent of the Company. Any unauthorized transfer of the SOFTWARE shall result in the immediate termination of this Agreement.

6.	**TERMINATION:** This license is effective until terminated. This license will terminate automatically without notice from the Company and become null and void if you fail to comply with any provisions or limitations of this license. Upon termination, you shall destroy the Documentation and all copies of the SOFTWARE. All provisions of this Agreement as to warranties, limitation of liability, remedies or damages, and our ownership rights shall survive termination.

7.	**MISCELLANEOUS:** This Agreement shall be construed in accordance with the laws of the United States of America and the State of New York and shall benefit the Company, its affiliates, and assignees.

8.	**LIMITED WARRANTY AND DISCLAIMER OF WARRANTY:** The Company warrants that the SOFTWARE, when properly used in accordance with the Documentation, will operate in substantial conformity with the description of the SOFTWARE set forth in the Documentation. The Company does not warrant that the SOFTWARE will meet your requirements or that the operation of the SOFTWARE will be uninterrupted or error-free. The Company warrants that the media on which the SOFTWARE is delivered shall be free from defects in materials and workmanship under normal use for a period of thirty (30) days from the date of your purchase. Your only remedy and the Company's only obligation under these limited warranties is, at the Company's option, return of the warranted item for a refund of any amounts paid by you or replacement of the item. Any replacement of SOFTWARE or media under the warranties shall not extend the original warranty period. The limited warranty set forth above shall not apply to any SOFTWARE which the Company determines in good faith has been subject to misuse, neglect, improper installation, repair, alteration, or damage by you. EXCEPT FOR THE EXPRESSED WARRANTIES SET FORTH ABOVE, THE COMPANY DIS-CLAIMS ALL WARRANTIES, EXPRESS OR IMPLIED, INCLUDING WITHOUT LIMITATION, THE IMPLIED WARRANTIES OF MERCHANTABILITY AND FITNESS FOR A PARTICULAR PURPOSE. EXCEPT FOR THE EXPRESS WARRANTY SET FORTH ABOVE, THE COMPANY DOES NOT WARRANT, GUARANTEE, OR MAKE ANY REPRESENTATION REGARDING THE USE OR THE RESULTS OF THE USE OF THE SOFTWARE IN TERMS OF ITS CORRECT-NESS, ACCURACY, RELIABILITY, CURRENTNESS, OR OTHERWISE.

IN NO EVENT, SHALL THE COMPANY OR ITS EMPLOYEES, AGENTS, SUPPLI-ERS, OR CONTRACTORS BE LIABLE FOR ANY INCIDENTAL, INDIRECT, SPECIAL, OR CONSEQUENTIAL DAMAGES ARISING OUT OF OR IN CONNECTION WITH THE LICENSE GRANTED UNDER THIS AGREEMENT, OR FOR LOSS OF USE, LOSS OF DATA, LOSS OF INCOME OR PROFIT, OR OTHER LOSSES, SUSTAINED AS A RESULT OF INJURY TO ANY PERSON, OR LOSS OF OR DAMAGE TO PROPERTY, OR CLAIMS OF THIRD PARTIES, EVEN IF THE COMPANY OR AN AUTHORIZED REPRESENTATIVE OF THE COMPANY HAS BEEN ADVISED OF THE POSSIBILITY OF SUCH DAMAGES. IN NO EVENT SHALL LIABILITY OF THE COMPANY FOR DAMAGES WITH RESPECT TO THE SOFTWARE EXCEED THE AMOUNTS ACTUALLY PAID BY YOU, IF ANY, FOR THE SOFTWARE.

SOME JURISDICTIONS DO NOT ALLOW THE LIMITATION OF IMPLIED WAR-RANTIES OR LIABILITY FOR INCIDENTAL, INDIRECT, SPECIAL, OR CONSEQUENTIAL DAMAGES, SO THE ABOVE LIMITATIONS MAY NOT ALWAYS APPLY. THE WARRANTIES IN THIS AGREEMENT GIVE YOU SPECIFIC LEGAL RIGHTS AND YOU MAY ALSO HAVE OTHER RIGHTS WHICH VARY IN ACCORDANCE WITH LOCAL LAW.

ACKNOWLEDGMENT

YOU ACKNOWLEDGE THAT YOU HAVE READ THIS AGREEMENT, UNDER-STAND IT, AND AGREE TO BE BOUND BY ITS TERMS AND CONDITIONS. YOU ALSO AGREE THAT THIS AGREEMENT IS THE COMPLETE AND EXCLUSIVE STATEMENT OF THE AGREEMENT BETWEEN YOU AND THE COMPANY AND SUPERSEDES ALL PROPOS-ALS OR PRIOR AGREEMENTS, ORAL, OR WRITTEN, AND ANY OTHER COMMUNICA-TIONS BETWEEN YOU AND THE COMPANY OR ANY REPRESENTATIVE OF THE COMPANY RELATING TO THE SUBJECT MATTER OF THIS AGREEMENT.

Should you have any questions concerning this Agreement or if you wish to contact the Company for any reason, please contact in writing at the address below or call the at the telephone number provided.

PTR Customer Service
Prentice Hall PTR
One Lake Street
Upper Saddle River, New Jersey 07458
Telephone: 201-236-7105

CD-ROM Description
and Installation Instructions ≡

The CD-ROM includes:

- FrameViewer, an application for reading documents on line in the viewer 5 directory
- The FrameMaker files used to create this book (in the rmf_win, rmf_mac, and rmf_unix directories)
- HTML versions of the files for this book in rmf_web
- Sample FrameMaker templates (described in the tempinfo.mif file in the template directory)

Minimum System Requirements

The hardware and software requirements to use FrameViewer are described below.

For a Macintosh computer

- Macintosh computer with a 68020 processor and 5 MB of RAM
- A hard disk with 5 MB of free space
- Macintosh System 7.0 or later
- A 13-inch monitor or PowerBook display

For a Windows-compatible system

- A computer with an 80386 processor and 8 MB of RAM
- A hard disk with 5 MB of free space
- Windows 3.1 and DOS 5.0 or later
- A VGA monitor and a mouse compatible with Windows 3.1

To Install FrameViewer on a Macintosh Computer

1. Insert the CD-ROM and double-click the FrameViewer Installer icon found in the VIEWER5 directory.
2. Follow the instructions in the Installer program to complete installation.

≡

To start FrameViewer, double-click the FrameViewer icon. To begin viewing the book files, open the "start" file in the rmf_mac directory and begin navigating from there.

To Install FrameViewer for the Windows Platform

1. Insert the CD-ROM into the drive.
2. Choose Run from the File menu in the Program Manager.
3. In the text box, type D:\Viewer5\Windows\Setup.exe and click OK. If your CD-ROM drive is not D, type the letter for your drive instead.
4. In the FrameViewer 5 installation dialog box, choose Registered Owner Version.
5. Follow the instructions in the Installer program to complete the installation.

To start FrameViewer, double-click the Frame-Viewer icon in the Program Manager. To begin viewing the book files, open the "start" file in the rmf_win/content directory and begin navigating from there.

To Install FrameViewer on a Solaris 2.x System

This product should be run only on a Solaris 2 system. You must run the installation script directly on the CD-ROM. To mount a CD-ROM, consult the documentation that came with your system or check with your system administrator.

1. To change to the CD-ROM directory, type cd/cdrom/rmf/viewer5/unix.
2. To run the CD-ROM installation script, type ./read.cd (include the initial period).

   Answer y to all y/n prompts.
3. When asked, provide the installation directory name. FrameViewer copies the appropriate installation files to your hard drive.
4. At the Frame Products Main Menu, type 1 (Basic Installation).
5. At the Basic Installation Menu, type 1 (Frame Viewer). When the menu reappears, type f (Finished Configuring Installation).
6. Type y to continue with the install, and type y again to confirm performing the script commands. FrameViewer copies the installation files to your directory, which takes several minutes.
7. Press Return when the installation is finished, and type q at the menu.

To start FrameViewer, type viewer at the system prompt. To view the book files, extract the contents of the file "book.tar" in the rmf_unix directory. Then use FrameViewer to open the "start" file and begin navigating from there.